CW00867576

Words from
the Heart

God has given me
a life of gifts

Tracy Elvina King

WESTBOW
PRESS®
A DIVISION OF THOMAS NELSON
& ZONDERVAN

WestBow Press books may be ordered through booksellers or by contacting:

WestBow Press
A Division of Thomas Nelson & Zondervan
1663 Liberty Drive
Bloomington, IN 47403
www.westbowpress.com
844-714-3454

Interior Image Credit: Walter and Luz Hoefflin

ISBN: 978-1-6642-1009-7 (sc)
ISBN: 978-1-6642-1010-3 (hc)
ISBN: 978-1-6642-1008-0 (e)

Library of Congress Control Number: 2020921290

Print information available on the last page.

WestBow Press rev. date: 11/17/2020

Dedication

I want to dedicate this book to my children, Eric and Brandon, and especially to my granddaughter Brenae, who inspired me every day to get up and move forward. I've strived for perfection, as well as giving it my all.

Writing this book gave me hope, and believing in my dreams. Besides, the unconditional love standing beside me. As I've told them, never give up, and always reach for the stars.

Love, Mom

Acknowledgement

The Author wishes to note,
with thanks and appreciation,
Thomas Nelson, Inc.,
Publisher of the
NEW KING JAMES VERISON,
for the use of
selected Bible verses
throughout her various chapters.
We are sincerely grateful - -

Tracy E. King

Contents

Words From The Heart

This book, **<u>Words From The Heart</u>**, is a story about how I found my way back to the light. It was not an easy road. These stories are my view of things I found, after peeling back the darkness, that was keeping me in bondage. I found Christ when the light came shining through, and my words came to me, because I had stories to tell.

There's no ending under God, even though these are the stories of my life's struggles. My battles of the love, I have for Christ. It seems, these stories were stored up in a life time, and this was the birth of **<u>Words From The Heart</u>**.

I'm hoping to inspire someone. I hope one of these stories helps someone find peace from stress in the mind and body. This book will hopefully ease any sorrow and pain in the heart. I hope you find yourself, and get to know Christ, for He can help your dreams and hopes become everlasting.

This book will encourage you to find faith, and ways to follow it. Did you know that it's not your eyes that see, but it's your heart. Blind faith is trust, and it takes courage to trust the unknown. I'm finding out my stories might not be the same as yours, but they're told from my heart. Perhaps you and I have something in common. We both are reaching for Christ. So, be blessed on your journey, and may your words flow as well, and I hope you enjoy my book.

Tracy Elvina King

Chapter 1

Going Forward With Encouragements

I want to give encouragement to all of you. You have so much success in you that you cannot fail, if you believe in yourself. Jesus knows how great you are. If you are worthy, and it matters not that in man's eyes, that you have not succeeded. Looking through Christ's eyes, you have accomplished your goals and pleased the Father. The unbelievers can't see your heart, and soul, they judge your shell. Always look at the positive side, you can find strength, and be strong. It's not the shell that needs cover, but the creation within of God.

You must carry trust that Christ is with you, if you carry love for the Father. As it says in **1 John 4:18 NKJV *There is no fear in love; but perfect love casts out fear, because fear involves torment. But he who fears has not been made perfect in love.** Jesus is guiding the journey. Don't be afraid, stand strong. The darkness, that comes and carries the disappointment, and tries to discourage, cannot walk on the Holy Mountain. Know this, God has a right hand and it protects you. Never doubt God or the Son, because to doubt them is to doubt you.

Failure is not an option, it's a choice. Think of all you have overcome. Battles you have fought, and won and obstacles you have braved. Still, you moved forward, winning victory after victory and by moving forward, and standing firm saying, **NO!** I will not give up. This is my journey, and my destiny. **I will succeed!** I can see very clearly.

If someone says just cry, I will smile. If it gets hard to walk, making it difficult to move forward, I will not scream, but

I will sing out loud songs of praise. Thanks to my Father in heaven. So, don't try to imagine yourself winning, see yourself winning. You have what God gave you to win. Never look back, keep looking forward, because what's behind you is done and what's in front of you is the journey you want to complete.

Never worry about things, if you know the job your doing is good for your heart, and soul. Under Christ, who is guiding you, always just go right, because there are no left turns. You need not to move around, but just stand still. Jesus will be standing with you and fighting alongside you. When you strive, don't move fast and pass up your neighbor. Always give encouragement. Remember, it all works well as a team. You hold Him up, and He holds you up, for if you are alone, there's no one to help you stand.

If you should fall from your blessings, you don't see, you just have to have faith. Sometimes the unknown causes confusion to the unbelievers, but if you believe, we pray through it, because heaven makes sense. I found failure only to be a word, and it can be erase. When the storm comes, and the waves are high, and it grows dark, and it seems your ship will sink, stop shaking, waiting to go down. Remember, who the captain is, **God!** Look, too, who is the crew standing with you, **Jesus!** This means you are protected, and after you've landed, you will be prepared for anything that comes your way. God has a plan, yes life deals challenges, but we overcome them with blessings. You must recognize them when you receive them. Don't look for more than you need, because it is called greed.

God would not bless you with more than you need, nor will He give you less than you need. Jesus guides, and God plants, just let yourself be open minded, because you are a creation from God. It matters not who you are, you're beautiful. There are no flaws in God's work. It's always perfect, only the work of man has imperfections. So, take a deep breath, and feel the breath of God. See and feel everything, relax! Heaven is near. **No!** Don't look down. Evil is conquered. There's nothing under your feet but dust. You must always choose to go right. The victory belongs to God, who blesses us for a job well done. On the left, you cannot see. There is no path to follow, but to the right the sun shines bright, and the path is clear. The only left I recognize is God's, for He raises His left hand to stop the storm, while blessing with His right.

This gives me peace within my soul, and my spirit is at rest. So I say, move forward, and know Jesus is guiding you home. On your journey, you only lose the weight sin has put on your back, trying to hold you here in chains. So, break free by walking the path. Evil may fellow but can't touch you, so free your mind, it's an illusion, and there is no cliff. Walk in faith and believe.

*Two are better than one, because they have a good reward for their labor.
*For if they fall, one will lift up his companion. But woe to him is alone when he falls, for
He has no one to help him up. Ecclesiastes 4:9-10 NKJV

A Blessing Shared:

Everyone deserves a blessing, and I believe when you receive a blessing, it should be shared with others. So, the world will continue to grow. When I receive a blessing, I want to share it with you.

* "If you abide in Me, and My words abide in you, you will ask what you desire, and it
shall be done for you. John 15:7 NKJV

3

*But now, thus says The LORD, who created you, O Jacob, and He who formed you, O
Israel: "Fear not, for I have redeemed, you; I have called you by your name; You are
mine. Isaiah 43:1 NKJV

Chapter 2

Don't Let Scars Keep You From Christ

Sometimes, memories can be hard to think about. Scars are sometimes painful and are so brutal, they hurt. They are too painful to remember, and so shameful, we keep them buried deep inside. Memories weigh you down. You don't want anyone to know, but I want you to know, God knows, this is why He sent Jesus, for Jesus can guide you. I know you've heard all this before, you're tired of sermons, and empty promises. What I'm telling you is everyone has scars that remind us what evil is capable of doing. The memory of this keeps us from hoping and dreaming of love and peace.

We don't see a future, and we are afraid to trust. We are also afraid of the storm that comes in the night. It leaves scars, God knows of your fears, and He sent His only Son to step in the path of evil, and take the pain. I trust that if I stand behind Jesus, with faith, and with all my hopes and dreams, I will overcome all obstacles put before me. I find, when I pray before I start my day, and before I close my eyes at night, it keeps the weight off my shoulders. I also find the more I pray, the harder evil works to try and keep me from Jesus. It means, if evil has to work harder than prayer is working.

If you put your heart's focus on Jesus, your scars will fad. I understand why you are not sure where to put your faith. God understands as well. Let me tell you of my experience. When I was standing where you are, I was doing nothing but existing on an empty shell. Holding on to scars, only makes you empty inside.

Sadly, you can't move forward, or backward. It makes you feel alone, scared to show yourself, fearful that someone will see the ugly scars. I found my strength to turn to the right, and look to Jesus. I saw the promises, and began to feel complete. I was feeling full with life, not hollow, inside. I was not alone, but loved. All you have to do is just turn right, **NO**, not left, just face right.

Don't let evil dictate how your life will be, and don't hold on to the scars, they're not souvenirs. I found that teachers aren't supposed to be brutal, and if you find yourself in the dark, you want to walk with a friend. They care enough to walk you to the light, and when things get rough, Jesus will stand by you. Jesus will hold your hand the whole time, guiding you to the light of glory. He will never leave you in the dark. I'm testifying, how I freed myself from my scars. How did I find the light of Jesus? He does not frown, saying you're late, but He does open His arms with love.

How can I tell you about others, if I have not experience the glory myself? I can't talk about someone, unless I know them well. I know Jesus, and when I look in the mirror, I no longer see scars, I only see beauty. I no longer feel empty. I was freed by faith. I say, every life saved, is a victory. If there are more than three souls saved, don't be discourage the victory is bigger than you know. Good and love is taking over, that's why evil is working overtime. That tells me, loving our neighbors is working. I'm not discouraged, I just keep looking right, and I find myself saying a verse from the Bible.

*For I am not ashamed of the gospel of Christ, for it is the power of God to salvation for
everyone who believes, for the Jew first and also for the Greek. Romans 1:16 NKJV

Yes, I'm not only testifying but living my dreams. I have hope for my future with Jesus. Many others were standing where you are. They found their way to Christ. You must know, you're not the only one who came to Mount Sinai. Others with scars, found Jesus late in life. Repent, asking the Father for forgiveness and mercy.

They saw the love to the right. I don't believe Christ looks at the time you came. **You're here!** I'm telling you my story, so you know, you have a choice. Others have scars, and evil clouds their sight, so they can't see there's a path to the right. If you just turn right, everything becomes clear. I found when things are clear, for me that the Bible was right, evil is a master of disguises.

Evil is the king of lies, nothing he does is for the good of mankind. It's a part of his makeup, selfish and all for his gain. When he speaks, he disguises the sound, so it sounds positive. In truth, it's not what it appears to be, only evil.

God knows, we get confuse. This is why He sent Jesus to guide us from evil, and take all our burdens away. Jesus will carry all of us, to give man a chance to repent. We should focus on prayer, and putting our heart "**right**." He also gives man the tools to go forward, and spread the word of Christ. Always give a hand to our neighbors. This world is supposed to be as it is in heaven.

*Do not love the world or the things in the world. If anyone loves the world, the love of the
Father is not in him. 1 John 2:15 NKJV

*Faithful are the wounds of a friend, but the kisses of an enemy are deceitful.
Proverbs 27:6 NKJV

As soon as man recognizes the true meaning of Christ, we can all be at peace, and evil will be no more cast out, as he was in heaven. Yes, I know you say, I've heard all this before. I am laying it out word by word, so you may understand it better. I'm telling you my story, and this is my testimony, how I was lost, and found my way back. As I said, everyone has scars, evil does not like beauty, that's why it's always dark.

It makes you only see scars and ugliness. There are no roses to perfume the air, no sunrise to make you smile, and birds don't sing the gospel. Most of all, there's no love, there's no one who cares, if you rise or fall. What lies in the dark is not your neighbor, and when walking, you are always alone. With no encouragement and promises build on lies, you only encounter walls that are really not there.

Have you seen the rain that never seems to stop? With no umbrella for cover, let me ask you. Does any of this sound familiar? Well, I've seen this, the bondage is real, but not impossible to break. You will, need help, someone like Christ.

***The fear of the LORD is the beginning of knowledge, but fools despise wisdom and
instruction. Proverbs 1:7 NKJV**

Christ, who stands with you, makes you feel that you are never alone. There are those who don't wish to walk to the right, looking always for ways to hurt and disrupt. These are people we pray for, no matter what. A good heart and soul never turns away from someone lost. Are you in need of love, no one is denied a chance to have Christ in their lives.

Remember, man is not a god, but we are His servant's, and His vessel. We follow His will, carrying on as Jesus did, for He left us a guide line. Even though the path is not easy, we don't walk alone. My Pastor once said in a sermon, that we should surround ourselves with positive things and people. So, when going out to serve the Lord, we remain positive in words and action.

You may think you know yourself better than I, but God knows you better than you. You should know yourself, and prayer tells you with love, to look pass the scars. Look through the mist created by evil, so you can't see. I realize when wounds heal, there may be scars, but they fade with Jesus. He absorbs all, leaving you healed physically and mentally.

I, myself, don't have any more scars, and I have no more weariness. My peace of mind is glorified, because I am no longer alone. I have Jesus, who will walk with me always. You need to know Jesus walks with all mankind. He can't help, if you don't believe or except Him.

Let's put it this way. If your mind believes, and told your body there was no air, you would begin to struggle to breathe. No matter what, someone did or said, wouldn't help if you believe, there was no air. Even, though you should be able to do so, if you truly believe in Jesus, than He can help.

As I said before, don't let the scars make you think you're not, worthy, or beautiful. Don't let evil win, find your strength, and stand up and be who God says you are. You ask me who am I? My answer would be, I am the child of God. My Father's name is Jehovah-Jireh, and He is my provider, and I have no more scars.

<u>Be Blessed On Your Journey</u>

Chapter 3

The Four Letter Word-Love

I want to tell you about a four letter word, **Love.** There are times we take advantage of this word, not fully understanding its meaning. There are some that are truly in the dark, and need knowledge and guidance. Some use it as a way to gain from it, and it is also to do good and bad. It's also used as comfort to someone, or to encourage someone. It's also used to physically hurt, or mentally to destroy the word. It is very important in man's world. That word again is **Love,** a word that is so important, it can build up, or tear down. There are a lot of positive ways we use it.

Love for a mother or father.
Love for a sister or brother.
Love for a husband or wife.
Love for a child.
Additionally, love of thy neighbor, and love thy self.
Most of all, love for Jehovah-Jireh, and the Son, Jesus.

Love is part of man's makeup, because it makes us move forward, whether it's for good or bad. Love is very powerful, and should be used carefully. It should be used with care of the heart. Love can take you down a dark road, because love is that powerful.

I realize you might think that love is good, but it depends on how you use it. Once, I started trying to get back to the path to Jesus. I really started seeing clearly the word love, and its meaning. Love can make you steal, and love can make you hate.

This kind of love is dark. If you look closer, this love wears a disguise. Lies are a seeker, and there's a hidden desire, because this love puts money first.

This love only sees material things. This love carries only pride, and does not humble. This love is selfish, and is only capable of loving itself. If unrighteous, I'm not trying to discourage you from love, but tell you how it can be used. Love is so powerful it should be handle with care of the heart under, the guidance of Jehovah.

We must stand up, and take control of our love. If in prayer, we, as God's children, we must not let evil provoke our love. We will not show fear, as written in the scripture.

*There is no fear in love; but perfect love casts out fear, because fear involves torment.
But he who fears has not been made perfect in love. 1 John 4:18 NKJV

We must find strength from the heavens. Besides, we must reach inside ourselves, and find our love given by God. We must give our love to God in His care, and follow the path of Jesus to the Father. We must keep a spiritual connection with Jehovah.

Remember, pray day and night, when we love, we must use our inner love from the heart and soul. It has been cleansed with the blood of Jesus.

*Hatred stirs up strife, but love covers all sins. Proverbs 10:12 NKJV

You must look at the whole thing, not half. You must look inside yourself, and ask, "What love do you carry within your heart?" If you love someone, do you do it for their inner self, or possessions you can get for gain, or their kindness? As I said, love is good and kind, but it depends on how and why you use it. There are those who only pray, telling God of their love, because they need it at that moment. It's called, a quick fix. We must go back and re-learn the word love, and what is its true meaning. Do you know? We must use this powerful word with care.

Love is a small word, but it carries a lot of power. It has so much power, it can cripple you, and has been known to drive a man to take their own life. We must take back control with prayer. We can't let evil take this beautiful, wonderful word, born for good, and turn it against us. Some would say, those people who took their lives, were just weak, not worthy. I don't believe it. They were just missed guided.

They might be lost, but with a kind hand, be saved, because love comes from the Lord. Real love can save those who are lost. We give to them the belief and hope, with that, it helps man find faith. Some men were never shown real love. So, when they came face to face with it, instead of embracing it, they treat it like an enemy. They don't know how to treat, and are afraid to believe there is hope. We must step forward, and show true love, with care. This way, they can begin to find love, and the path to Jesus. This brings hope.

Remember what real love is:

***Love suffers long and is kind; love does not envy; love does not parade itself, is not
puffed up;**

*does not behave rudely, does not seek its own, is not provoked, thinks no evil;
*does not rejoice in iniquity, but rejoices win the truth;
*bears all things, believes all things, hopes all things, endures all things.
*Love never fails. But whether there are prophecies, they will fail; whether there are
tongues, they will cease; whether there is knowledge, it will vanish away.
1 Corinthians 13: 4-8 NKJV

Forgiveness in love is the way of the Lord, Jehovah-Jireh. Love conquers, and I believe, love has moved mountains, and I believe, love calms the sea. Love protects against the storm. I believe true love can be strong as the amour of God. Love is God. I hope you have, or have found this love, and stayed strong with prayer.
Under Jehovah's love, you find a safe home, with a feeling of peace. In your heart, you get the sense of security, this love feels like home. Jehovah takes His love, and builds the Kingdom that we will inherit one day.

The knowledge of love has been revealed to man. We just have to stop and read the Holy Bible. It is full of wonder, and God's wisdom. If you believe in the journey, it is amazing how one small word could have so much power. We carry love with in ourselves. The love we use should build up, but never destroy. I have embraced the love under Jehovah. Using prayer, and with His love, there will be no disguises or hidden desires. Only love, and with this love we pray day and night.

My prayer would be like this:

"Lord, I ask for forgiveness, and mercy, and I will bow down, and surrender all to You. My heart, and soul is Yours. I cast out all others. I put you first Lord, I keep nothing for myself. You are my Savior, and my refuge. In You, I have found my love.
I thought it was lost, only to realize, it was I who was lost. I have found my way back to the path, Lord. I light candles with Your love. Thank You for my passage. I will work hard to show I'm worthy of Your love, even if it takes a life time. Lord, seeing true love has set me free. Amen"

So, I say to you, use love on the right side, and don't let evil control your beauty and stay blessed.

Chapter 4

The Man In The Church

There was a man, who was raised in Church, a faithful member, and believer in the Heavenly Father. Over the years, his health was declining. He was becoming weak from age, and other things. He was also losing his eye sight, and having trouble reading his Bible. This was the only thing that bothered him. You should know, too, that he was very faithful in his Bible studies. He lived a distance from his Church, where he had been a member all his life. It was starting to get harder to make the trip, but baring the pain he went to Church. After the services, he always felt light hearted, and whole. He also lost all his family, and some friends. Alone in the sense, he was not sad but at peace. God's love gave him comfort in his heart. God filled the void, so he never felt the loneliness.

He only had two wishes which he only spoke to God about. It was a hope and a dream. He prayed, both in Church and at night before, retiring. He has prayed this prayer for years, but he was not disappointed or discouraged. He believes in Christ, and God knows what's best for him. He continued to live in the word of God, and doing His will.

*And in that day you will say: "O Lord, I will praise You; Though You were angry with
me, Your anger is turned away, and You comfort me.
*Behold, God is my salvation, I will trust and not be afraid; For YAH, the LORD, is my
strength and song; He also has become my salvation."'
Isaiah 12:1-2 NKJV

Living the path God has set for him. His neighbors said, he is a god send, and so helpful. As the years went by, it was getting more difficult to help them. So, he would sit on the porch, and send out prayers to his neighbors. The man was very kind and had a good heart.

One day, on his way to church, he stopped four times to rest, before continuing. Church members were concern for him, and offered him a ride home. He let them know he appreciate their kindness, but said, "God is blessing me with strength to walk." The man wanted only to continue with his regular routine.

On the way home one day, he notice a small church, and wonder why he never seen it before? Could it be a blessing from God? This church was just down the way. So, he decide, he would visit the small church the following Sunday. However, everyone at his regular church became concern, when he missed that

Sunday. Even the Pastor was worried, because he never missed a Sunday. The man never thought it would cause such a panic. To check on him, the Pastor, and congregation, showed up at his home. With sadness in his voice and his heart, he explained why he had missed Church. Everyone started talking at once. Someone said, "You can ride with us." Someone else said. "No! We can share." It was so touching, and over whelming, he started to cry.

Once again, he declined. He said, "The blood of Jesus lets me get to Church on my own." He did say, if at any time he needed help, he promised to call and visit when he could. The congregation understood, but was still concern, and sad to see him go. After everyone left, the Pastor stayed, and prayed with him. Though the Congregation wished he would have stayed.

He repeated his wishes, and then went inside his home feeling sad. Consoling himself, he was reminding himself that he was not losing his friends, not moving away, but was still going to be worshiping and living the will of God. He was just moving closer to home.

After he joined the new Church, he began getting weaker. He wasn't able to stand for long, or raise his arms high. His site was worse, but he was happy, because he knew most of the scriptures by memory. With a smile in his heart every day, he still asked God for the two things he most wanted.

Every Sunday, at the new church, the man always set down in the same row, and in the same seat. He had been attending the Church for 2 years, and he still asked God for the two things he most wanted: **Strength to get around, and a family to love.**

He always prayed, and thanked God for life. The man started to believe, not that God didn't hear his prayers, but that God was waiting for him to come home, to His Kingdom. His family

17

would be there, and that made him smile, in his heart and soul. He knew there was no sickness there, and that both his wishes would come true. God's love also shines on His faithful followers, and is merciful. God has powers no one else has, and we must believe in His healing.

*If any of you lacks wisdom, let him ask of God, who gives to all liberally and without
reproach, and it will be given to him. James 1:5 NKJV

*You will keep him in perfect peace, whose mind is stayed on You, because he trusts in
You. Isaiah 26:3 NKJV

The story continues of the man in his new church, where he attended every Sunday, and listened to the Pastor and Choir. Each week, he also sat in the same seat. The congregation wondered why he would come to Church, if he's just going to sit there.

One Sunday, the Pastor asked the congregation to stand, and said to the man, "We are truly blessed you are here, and what you mean to us." Everyone was telling their stories, while the man sat silent. When it came time for him to share, it took him a while to stand. He began to tell his story.

<u>He said ...</u>
"My eyes don't work that well, and my hands are weak, and my legs hurt every day. It's hard to stand, but with God's help, I'm able to come to Church. I thank Him for helping me get here. I asked God, if He could bless me with a family. I thanked Him, and praised Him. I now realized He heard my prayers before I even asked. He gave me you as a family. So, although I just sit here. My heart is smiling. My soul

is bigger. My faith is stronger than ever before, Christ is guiding my spirit."

You see, God does bless us, and when we speak, He does hear us. He even knows our thoughts, and pain. He is working on all things. It's just not at our speed. Remember, sometimes you may not get a prayer, because God knew that it would be more harmful than helpful. God gives us tools to work on things ourselves.

He does not leave us, but watches over us as our protector. Sometimes when He steps in, He has already fixed the problem, and granted our prayers with a blessing. You may not have noticed because you are not looking through God's eyes, but through the eyes of man.

You must keep faith. God does not pass over His faithful followers. He keeps all promises He's made. **If God said it, and it is written, than it is so!** The smile you saw on the old man's face, and the smile in his heart and soul, is yours.

Chapter 5

Inspiration For Mankind

We should be grateful for God sending us Jesus, and thankful for Jesus saving our lives. Can you name things, which you are thankful for, in your life? Things that inspire you, someone to believe and hope. If you think of more than ten, it's ok. God loves praises, and songs from the heart.

My Inspiration For Mankind-Faith:

Faith is what I have in Jesus. I don't need proof to believe. I don't need anything set before me, because my faith, is based on my love for the Father and the Son. I have faith, and with this faith, I can stand up, and face all obstacles in my path. I will not give up my faith. Jesus is before me, guiding the way, my faithful eyes are open.

*For by grace you have been saved through faith, and that not of yourselves; it is the gift
of God,
*not of works, lest anyone should boast. Ephesians 2:8-9
NKJV

My Inspiration For Mankind-Spirit:
My spirit gives me the confidence I have in myself. I will not be afraid, for Christ is my essence. My spirit has the ability to restore my faith, and love in the Holy Ghost.

*Now may the God of patience and comfort grant you to be like-minded toward one
another, according to Christ Jesus,
*that you may with one mind and one mouth glorify the God and Father of our Lord
Jesus Christ. Romans 15:5-6 NKJV

*For God has not given us a spirit of fear, but of power and of love and of a sound mind.
2 Timothy 1:7 NKJV

Inspiration For Mankind-Soul:

They say the soul is the window of man's inner being. I will have strength. My love for Christ is in my soul, I refuse to stand empty. My soul is restored, and my spiritual being as well. My soul will not let weakness lead me into darkness. I give my soul freely to Jesus for safe keeping.

* "Come to Me, all you who labor and are heavy laden, and I will give you rest.
* "Take My yoke upon you and learn from Me, for I am gentle and lowly in heart, and
you will find rest for your souls.
* "For My yoke is easy and My burden is light." Matthew 11:28-30 NKJV

My Inspiration For Mankind-Trust:

Having the trust in the Father, and knowing through Him, I can trust His Son, for Jesus is my path to the Father and the Kingdom. Trust means believing in something not visible to the eye, but visible to the heart. Trust is having the ability to hold on to that, and trusting it will get me to the place called home. My trust in the Son knows I can close my eyes, and walk around a corner blindly, and knowing Jesus will guide me safely, because I trust Him completely.

*When you pass through the waters, I will be with you; and through the rivers, they shall
not overflow you. When you walk through the fire, you shall not be burned, nor shall the
flame scorch you. Isaiah 43:2 NKJV

*Trust in the LORD with all your heart, and lean not on your own understanding;
*In all your ways acknowledge Him, and He shall direct your paths.
Proverbs 3:5-6 NKJV

My Inspiration For Mankind-Believe:

I think, without belief, we lose our link to God. There can't be a connection with Christ, if you don't believe. I believe in being strong, for I have the strength to take a stand, and not be turned around. I believe strongly that I don't stand alone. **I will have the victory!** I am a vessel that God uses, and God loves mankind.
This is what makes the difference between being strong, and being weak, having joy or sorrow, having strength or weariness. I believe I can overcome anything, because I believe in Jesus.

*You believe that there is one God. You do well. Even the demons believe--and tremble!
James 2:19 NKJV

*But without faith it is impossible to please Him, for he who comes to God must believe
that He is, and that He is a rewarder of those who diligently seek Him.
Hebrews 11:6 NKJV

My Inspiration For Mankind-Peace:

Thank you, Jesus for bringing peace from the Father to mankind. Peace gives man comfort and keeps the mind strong. There is no doubts what bleeds into the body, is a temple that houses what man use to fight evil. The weapon we will use is peace. We must have peace within us so, we can feel the joy.

* "These things I have spoken to you, that in Me you may have peace. In the world you
will have tribulation; but be of good cheer, I have overcome the world."
John 16:33 NKJV

* "The LORD bless you and keep you;
* The LORD make His face shine upon you, and be gracious to you;
* The LORD life up His countenance upon you, and give you peace."'
Numbers 6:24-26 NKJV
* "Peace I leave with you, My peace I give to you; not as the world gives do I give to you.
Let not your heart be troubled, neither let it be afraid. John 14:27 NKJV

My Inspiration For Mankind-Wisdom of God:

I thank God every day for giving mankind, the book of knowledge. They will need wisdom on this journey, to carry on, and have the wisdom to understand what's in front of them. This wisdom is not known to the unbelievers. Only revealed to the wise man, who can recite the commandments, and know their meaning. You must have enough wisdom to know God does not want you to fail. He wants you to reach your full potential in Christ.

*If any of you lacks wisdom, let him ask of God, who gives to all liberally and without
reproach, and it will be given to him.
*But let him ask in faith, with no doubting, for he who doubts is like a wave of the sea
driven and tossed by the wind.
*For let not that man suppose that he will receive anything from the Lord;
he is a double-minded man, unstable in all his ways. James 1:5-8 NKJV

My Inspiration For Mankind-Hope:

Hope is something that gives dreams, and these dreams, help us build on God's word. What gives us peace inside is that our hopes stand with Christ. Having hope, we reach out to God's path. Never be afraid to hope, because it's good for the soul. Hope can help set you free, and you can be inspired by it. Hope also gives confidence in one's self.

*For we were saved in this hope, but hope that is seen is not hope; for why does one still

hope for what he sees?
*But if we hope for what we do not see, we eagerly wait for it with perseverance.
Romans 8:24-25 NKJV

*Now may the God of hope fill you with all joy and peace in believing, that you may
abound in hope by the power of the Holy Spirit. Romans 15:13 NKJV

My Inspiration for Mankind-Man's Will:

Mankind has the will to withstand all that comes its way. Yes, we are human, and we are not gods. What man seems to forget, is Jesus is guiding us. With His love, we are very strong willed. We move forward, and mankind can take all his love, and faith and the will to face evil.
Never be afraid to say no, and to have the confidence in one's self. It is written, that there is no fear in love, so build on that. Your will can find its strength, and conquer all that evil puts in your way.

*But those who wait on the LORD shall renew their strength; They shall mount up with
wings like eagles, they shall run and not be weary, they shall walk and not faint.
Isaiah 40:31 NKJV

*For this is the will of God, that by doing good you may put to silence the ignorance of
foolish men-- 1 Peter 2:15 NKJV

*Restore to me the joy of Your salvation, and uphold me by Your generous Spirit.
Psalm 51:12 NKJV

My Inspiration For Mankind-Love:

I'm thankful God blessed the world, and loved mankind. He not only created man with careful love, but when man goes left, not right on the path, He still gives second chances. He gave the Kingdom love and good health.

God is love, and who ever lives in love, lives in God, and God in them.

*with all lowliness and gentleness, with longsuffering, bearing with one another in love,
Ephesians 4:2 NKJV

*And above all things have fervent love for one another, for *"love will cover a multitude* **of** *sins."* **1 Peter 4:8 NKJV**

*He who does not love does not know God, for God is love.
1 John 4:8 NKJV

*But you, beloved, building yourselves up on your most holy faith, praying in the Holy Spirit,
*keep yourselves in the love of God, looking for the mercy of our LORD Jesus Christ unto eternal life. Jude 1:20-21 NKJV

My Inspiration For Mankind-Heart:

The heart has compassion, for God the Father, and Jesus the Messiah. The heart is what feeds the mind, the spirit and soul. Faith makes the heart stronger, and gives peace and nourishment to the temple of man. Without heart, we become empty shells. We must find balance in this difficult world. I think the heart is a battery that sends love to the soul and spirit.

* "I will give you a new heart and put a new spirit within you; I will take the heart of
stone out of your flesh and give you a heart of flesh. Ezekiel 36:26 NKJV

*Create in me a clean heart, O God, and renew a steadfast spirit within me.
Psalm 51:10 NKJV

I'm giving you inspiration for your heart and spirit, as well as for the soul and mind. In this story, I have given you inspiration, to move forward. As you do, so will all your burdens and pain, and the sin will fall in the sea.

Be Blessed

Chapter 6

Jesus Walked With Me

This is a story of a young girl named Elizabeth, and her mother Mary, who is a housekeeper. Elizabeth was 10 years old, and had no friends at school. The kids teased her, because her clothes were worn and fade. So, when she was on the playground, she was always alone. She watched her classmates play, as she sat in a corner.

Her mother had told her to talk to Jesus. "Elizabeth, He can be a great friend, always loyal, and listens to all you say with no judgements, and He makes the heart feel loved." She tried, but the next day she was still sad. So, Elizabeth stopped talking to Jesus, because everything was still the same. Elizabeth was still feeling alone, and the kids never stopped teasing her.

* "If you abide in Me, and My words abide in you, you will ask what you desire, and it
shall be done for you. John 15:7 NKJV

On her 11th birthday, instead of toys, she got a pair of shoes, pants, and a shirt from the Salvation Army. She never had new clothes or toys, just a mother's love, which made her smile. Their apartment consisted of one bedroom and a bath, Elizabeth would sit at the window, and dream of a big house, a bike and clothes.

After her birthday, Elizabeth and her mother met a man named Luc. He seemed nice, but something kept pushing at Elizabeth's soul. She couldn't put a finger on it, but she was afraid of him. One reason was, it had always just been her and her mother. One day, Luc came to visit, and brought the meal. He brought steaks, potatoes, veggies and a cake. All her mother had to do was cook it. Her mother said that they needed to thank him. Elizabeth was excited, because she only normally got cake at Thanksgiving, Christmas or maybe on her birthday. However, it did nothing to change her feelings towards him.

Luc gave her mother some flowers, and she smiled. She never saw her mother look so happy. Elizabeth decide right there, she would not tell her mother her true feelings, about Luc. It was sad, because they never kept secrets from each other. When sitting down to eat, they had to push the table together along with the couch. They only had two chairs.

Elizabeth and her mother joined hands with Luc, to pray over the meal. He looked surprised, but took their hands. Elizabeth became very uncomfortable, when Luc, instead of holding her hand, continued to rub it. However, her mother never saw that. So, when they began the meal, Elizabeth was so confused, she could not eat.

After dinner, while her mother and Luc talked, Elizabeth sat by the window, looking out and wondering what she should do. There was no one to talk too about it. After he left, her mother ask her what was wrong. Elizabeth said, "I'm just happy for you." Her mother looked at her, and decided not to persuade it. The next day, while her mother was napping, she went to the bathroom. She noticed that the wall paper was loose by the sink. Trying to fix it, Elizabeth realized it was covering a small door. She pulled the paper back, and pushed the door open.

It was a small little room that she could fit in. Her mother called to her. So, closing the door, and pressing the paper back she left, only to see that Luc had returned. Putting her head down, she said, "Hello, nice to see you again."

He had been coming around for almost two months, and always touched her while eating. She noticed he would ask about her mother's schedule. He also inquired about who watched over her, when her mother is away. Although, her mother didn't share the same opinion as her, it still made Elizabeth uncomfortable, with his constant stairs.

*Behold, God is my salvation, I will trust and not be afraid; For YAH, the Lord, is my strength and my song; He also has become my salvation.'" Isaiah 12:2 NKJV

Since she had to walk alone to school and home, she became afraid. So, even though the kids teased her and called her names, she stayed close to them. It was safer that way. Elizabeth thought one day, that the girls were calling her name, but when she looked across the street, she saw Luc, standing there watching her. She pretended not to see him.

Her mother was napping when she got home, so Elizabeth started her homework. She had asked her teacher for some glue.

She wanted to fix the paper in the bathroom, over the door, but where she could still open it. After checking on her mother, she got a shirt her mother used for cleaning, soap and cleaned out the little room.

Now happy, she closed it, put the cleaning way, and she would keep the little room a secret. Later that evening, Luc was back, again, Elizabeth was feeling uncomfortable. After dinner Elizabeth sat by herself to pray to Jesus, this time with her heart.

"Jesus, what can I say? We go to church, and some are not kind to my mother and me. It's not the same as the Pastor says, "Our Father's house should be all good with love.

"I do feel safe when I'm there, but sad when I leave. I say my prayers before eating, also at lunch time at school. The kids just laugh, and call me strange. My mother said, You would answer all my prayers. I've been praying for material things, but I should be thanking You for myself and my mother's lives.

"I wonder why I'm afraid of this man? I don't want my mother unhappy, but I don't feel safe. Can You protect me, like it says in the Bible? I know the Bible well. It's the only book I have to read and it has stories of good conquering evil. I love all the stories. Well, it's time for bed. Thanks for listening. My mom was right, You do listen, and I feel much better, I don't feel alone anymore."

*Finally, my brethren, be strong in the Lord and in the power of His might.
*Put on the whole armor of God, that you may be able to stand against the wiles of the
devil. Ephesians 6:10-11 NKJV

*Therefore take up the whole armor of God, that you may be able to withstand in the evil
day, and having done all, to stand. Ephesians 6:13 NKJV

The next day, on the way to school, making sure to keep up with the kids, Elizabeth continued to look around for Luc. Then she saw him again. She was so distracted watching him, she walked into another man, by mistake. She said, "Sorry." He scared her, he held her arm tight, so she pulled away and ran to school. When Elizabeth got to school, she started praying in her mind.

"Thank You! Thank You! Jesus! I'm not sure how I got the courage to pull away, or the energy to run that far. I hope You never leave my side. Thanks for calming me down, I'm going to class now, Thank You."

* Be strong and of good courage, do not fear nor be afraid of them; for the LORD your
God, He is the One who goes with you. He will not leave you nor forsake you."
Deuteronomy 31:6 NKJV

After school, she followed the same routine, walking behind the others kids on the way home. Only two kids lived on her block. Once she got close to home, she saw her mother, who would always sit outside waiting for her. Today, Luc was there. She was wondering why, he was so early? He always came around dinner time. When she reached them, she noticed he had a bag. Her mother said, "How was your day?" Elizabeth kept looking down at her feet, but still said Hello to both of them. Luc said, "Hello, this is for you." She looked at her mother, and her mother said, "Its ok, say thank you." Elizabeth thanked Luc, but her mind was racing. She was 11 years old, and had never been given anything except clothes, shoes and a Bible.

When they went inside, her mother told her to open her gift. Her mother inquired, "What did you get?" There were three books. They were so beautiful, she never thought she would ever have some of her own. She read at school, but these books were hers. Although, she forgot to thank him, instead she only felt danger, so pure, it almost made her melt.

* "Be strong and of good courage, do not fear nor be afraid of them; for the LORD your
God, He is the One who goes with you. He will not leave you nor forsake you."
Deuteronomy 31:6 NKJV

Later, her mom invited him to stay for dinner, but Elizabeth was trying her best not to show fear. So, using the books for an excuse, not to make eye contact, she began to pray in her mind to Jesus.

I'm so afraid! What should I do? Should I tell my mother I'm afraid? I'm confused. Can You give me a sign of what to do? Are You really there listening? Is there a way You can reach down and hold me till it's safe?

*GOD is our refuge and strength, a very present help in trouble. Psalm 46:1 NKJV

Her time with Jesus ended, when her mother called her for dinner ...
"Thanks for listening. You've become a good friend."

After dinner, Luc stayed for a while, then left. The next day, after school, her mother was taking another nap. Elizabeth decided to fix up her little room in the bathroom. She found some old clothes that had been thrown away. She took her time washing them, and hung them in the tub.

After her nap, her mother asked her, "What are you going to do with these?" Elizabeth replied, "I'm going to make cushions with them." However, she didn't tell her mother that they were for her little room, because she wanted to keep it to herself. When it was time for bed, and after her prayers, she climb on the couch, and began to pray to Jesus in her mind.

"Jesus, are You ready to show me what to do? I'm more afraid today than yesterday. The Bible says, with just a word You can calm a storm. Well, I don't need that much power, but I do need You. Good night Jesus, I love You. You are my best friend."

The next day, Luc was back at the house, this time he hugged her. However, her mom didn't see him kiss her head. Later, after dinner, Elizabeth sat in her corner again, praying to Jesus.

I'm in need of You. My Pastor said, You protect all, if you believe. I believe, I believe with all my soul. You're quiet, is it because You're working on it? Can You speed it up a little? I'm sorry to rush You, but I'm so afraid."

The next day, while her mother napped, she put her cushion in the little room. Her mother had finished with a milk bottle. She cleaned it, and put water in it. Elizabeth put it in her little room, she would call it her club. The next day, going to school, she felt lighter, and couldn't say why. After school, she followed the same routine. After getting home, Luc came to visit, and brought her a big bag of cookies. She was thankful, but afraid. Luc said, "Do I get a hug and a kiss?"

Looking at her mother, she said, "It was fine." It was not with her. What would she do? Then, she would need to tell her mother everything. Every day, from then on, Elizabeth put two cookies in a jar she had. They were in her little room. One day, her mother said, she was going to be late coming home.

Two hours after school, Elizabeth was overwhelmed. She said to herself, "What am I supposed to do alone?" She was afraid Luc would come back, and she was by herself. That made her head hurt. She remembered her mother saying, "We have a routine."

That night, Elizabeth asked Jesus …
"Please be with me tomorrow, please!"

When she came home the next day, she did not see anyone, nor was there anyone in the house. So, she got her books, and went to her little room. She had a small flash light, that was only to be used if the lights went out. She didn't want to use up the batteries. She also had a cross, her mother made her. Her little room was nice.

"Thank You Jesus for making sure I got home safely. Are You working to make sure that Luc doesn't come while my mother is away? I never was afraid when my mother was going to be late, but now I am not sure why I'm afraid of Luc.

"I feel danger, and I wanted to say, I'm sorry Jesus, I didn't pray to You before. I hope You know You have become my best friend. I think my mother's home. I just heard the door. Wait! There's someone else here!"

She turned the flash light off, and stayed quiet. Whoever was in the house was moving around. If it was her mother, she would have already called out to her.

"Oh Jesus, Oh Jesus, there is someone in the bathroom. Who is it? I can tell by the smelled, it's Luc! That's his smell, and what is he doing here? How did he get in? Jesus, please don't let him find me.

*I WILL lift up my eyes to the hills--from whence comes my help?
*My help comes from the LORD, who made heaven and earth. Psalm 121:1-2 NKJV

He kept moving around. Then he finally left. Elizabeth decided to wait for her mother to come home, so she stayed in her little room. Then, she heard her mother Mary, call her name, and Elizabeth came out of her small space. She found her mother putting away food, and she was alone. She walked to her mother, and held her tight. "What's wrong?" asked her mother. Elizabeth immediately broke into tears. Before she could respond, there was a knock at the door. Her mother went to answer it, it was Luc.
He told Mary, he had come by, but no one answered the door. Mary told him, that her daughter was never to answer the door when she was alone. When her mother looked at her, for the first time she lied. He knew she was not there, or so he thought. Elizabeth said, "I was afraid, I heard a noise, so I went to our neighbors. I'm sorry I worried you." He smiled, and hugged her. Later, after he left, her mother said, she was staying home a few days. When they went to bed, and while her mother slept, she prayed to Jesus.

"I'm sorry I lied, please forgive me, and please don't give up on me. I'm not sure what to do? I feel lost Jesus. The Bible says, You are working on all things. Can You work on mine, I'm scared. Jesus, thanks for Your understanding."

On Saturday, there was no school. Sitting at the window, praying to Jesus, her mom thought she was reading.

Instead, she was asking Jesus …
"What can I do about what's happening? I can run away somewhere far when we go to church. I'll go then. I'm sorry Jesus, I'm scared. I will always pray to You, because Your my only friend, and You have become a part of my life."

*Now may the God of hope fill you with all joy and peace in believing, that you may
abound in hope by the power of the Holy Spirit. Romans 15:13 NKJV

The next morning, getting ready for Church, her mother asked, why she had her backpack. Elizabeth answered, "I have my books and Bible in it." Her mother said, "Ok, make sure you don't leave it there." She did not lie, but just didn't say she was running away. "I'm glad my mother didn't look inside my backpack." On the way to Church, her mother's friend, Luc, stop them. He asks where they were going. Her mother said, "To Church." Elizabeth kept her head down, even when her mother said, he was welcome to join them.
Elizabeth saw him look away and say, "Not today, maybe another time." Although her head was down, when he looked at her, she now knew she had to run away. I'm going to miss my mom, she said.

<u>When they got to Church she prayed hard to Jesus ...</u>
"Can You watch over my mother while I'm gone? I wish I could take You, but I need someone to look after her."

When Church was over, her mother said, "I have a surprise for you. I wanted to wait until today to tell you, I'm taking you to McDonald's." Her eyes got waded opened, and her mouth dropped. She had never, in my life, been to McDonald's. Her mom laughed and said, "Come on my angel."

*For I know the thoughts that I think toward you, says the LORD, thoughts of peace and
not of evil, to give you a future and a hope. Jeremiah 29:11 NKJV

When they got to McDonald's and sat down to eat, her mother said, "My housekeeping job with the family is going to get better. They are also planning to move to New York, and they want to take us with them. We will be leaving Friday." As they sat there, her mother also said, she need time to pack and clean. "We will have a small house and you will have your own room. So, how do you feel about that?" Elizabeth just sat there stunned, and stared.

<u>She said to herself ...</u>
"This is a blessing. I know it was You Jesus. You reached out and blessed us. Thank You, I won't stop praying to You, because You are coming with us, right? I need You!"

Her mother asked her again, "How do you feel, happy or sad to go?" She said, "This is like Christmas!" Her mom laughed, and said, "I'm glad you're happy. We'll spend the next few days together. I'm helping the family pack. Since you are out of school, would you like to help me pack for the family?" Elizabeth said, "Yes! I will work hard, and be real careful. I don't want to stay alone." "Ok, we are a team.," her mother said. After they got home, Luc came over for dinner. When her mother told him of the new job, he appeared angry. Elizabeth kept her head down while, her mother told him, "It's my job. I'm sorry we have to go, but you can come and visit." Luc got up and left, without saying a word. Her mother seemed sad, but Elizabeth was still afraid.

"Jesus! Is it ok? Will he come back? He was really mad, and his eyes were hateful. What do we do if he does come back?"

*He who dwells in the secret place of the Most High shall abide under the shadow of the
Almighty.
*I will say of the Lord, "He is my refuge and my fortress; May God, in Him I will trust."
Psalm 91:1-2 NKJV

*He shall cover you with His feathers, and under His wings you shall take refuge; His
truth shall be your shield and buckler. Psalm 91:4 NKJV

When they went to bed, Elizabeth waited till her mother went to sleep. She got up, and looked out the window. There was Luc, parking his car, and walking towards the building. She immediately woke up her mother.
She said, **"Trust me mama, and come with me, please!"** **"What's wrong? What happened?,"** her mother asked. **"Please! Trust me, we need to go! Please!"** Elizabeth said.
Her mother saw the fear in her eyes, and that she was afraid. She followed her to the bathroom, and there she opened the door

39

to the small room. Her mother looked surprised. **"Please, we have to get in there!"** Her Mother looked at her, and climbed in. Elizabeth followed her and closed the door. **"Quiet mama, listen."**

They heard the front door open. They held each other tight. Luc was moving around the house, and came into the bathroom, while Elizabeth prayed to Jesus.

"Please, don't let him find me and my mother."

Her mother then realized who was in their home. Thinking they were gone, Luc stayed for a while, waiting to see when they would return. They never made a sound. Sometime later he left, but the sun was up. They quickly packed their clothes and pictures. It was all they had. But luckily, her mother said, they could stay with the family.

*You shall not be afraid of the terror by night, nor of the arrow that flies by day.
*Nor of the pestilence that walks in darkness, nor of the destruction that lays waste at
noonday. Psalm 91:5-6 NKJV

So, they left, to take a bus. They would not feel safe until they were on the plane. Luc was parked down the street, waiting for them. He got out of the car, and angrily stepped in front of her mother. He said, "Where have you been? And, where are you going? You're not leaving!" Elizabeth kept her head down. "I need to get to work!," said her mother. Luc responded, "Why do you have suit cases?" Her mother said, "That's our bus!"
Her mother had been catching the bus for years to go to work. Elizabeth had no idea her mother had friends on the bus. When the bus came to a stop, Luc again stepped in front of them. "You

have to stay with me!" When the bus door opened, the driver, and another passenger asked, if they needed help?

The driver and the passenger called her mother by name. Her mother looked at the passenger and said, "No, we got this." Luc reluctantly stepped out of their way, but stood staring, as they got on the bus. As the bus drove away, Luc continued to stare at them. Elizabeth raised her head, looking into his face. She saw pure evil, like the Bible talks about.

* "The LORD will fight for you, and you shall hold your peace." Exodus 14:14 NKJV

*No weapon formed against you shall prosper, and every tongue which rises against you
in judgement you shall condemn. This is the heritage of the servants of the LORD, and
their righteousness is from Me," says the Lord. Isaiah 54:17 NKJV

She asked Jesus …
"Is it over? Are we safe and free?"

Later, they arrived at her mother's work. She helped clean and pack. Her mother's employer said, they could stay until Friday. She never told her mother, that when she took the trash out at their new place, she saw Luc sitting in his car.

She quickly looked away, and in her mind asked Jesus …
"Will he get in? Do You think they have an alarm or two big dogs?"

*But I will sing of Your poser; Yes, I will sing aloud of Your mercy in the morning; for

You have been my defense and refuge in the day of my trouble. Psalm 59:16 NKJV

When Friday came, they planned to leave early. Her mother helped with the last of the packing and cleaning. They finally climbed into a cab. Elizabeth was so relieved and happy, she cried. Her mother knew why, and hugged her tight. She told her, she loved her. Luc, without their knowledge, was following them close behind. Elizabeth again spoke to Jesus in her mind, as her mother held her tight.

"Thank You for protecting us from harm. I have studied the Bible, and You are so merciful, and powerful with love. I realize gratefulness has no limits, and if one just believes, the blessings You give, are like being wrap in love."

They arrived at the airport. Elizabeth saw all the planes. She was so overwhelmed to be safe, and free from evil. She never knew fear until she met her mother's friend, Luc. After checking their luggage in, which wasn't much, they sat, waiting to board.

She said to her mother, "I'm sorry about what happened mama. I know he made you happy." Her mother used both hands to lift her face up, and looking Elizabeth in the eyes, said, "You make me happy, and when it's time, God will let me know, and send someone special." Elizabeth smiled because, it sounded wonderful. It was time to board.

She walked beside her mother with her head held high. She was only 11 years old, but she had Christ with her. When Elizabeth looked back, there was Luc. She did not put her head down, nor did she fear him. With calm and courage, she walked up the steps to the plane, and remembered two verses.

*Though I walk in the midst of trouble, you will revive me;
You will stretch out Your
hand against the wrath of my enemies, and Your right hand
will save me.
Psalm 138:7 NKJV

*But Jesus looked at them and said to them, "With men this
is impossible, but with God
all things are possible." Matthew 19:26 NKJV

They both smiled, when they arrived in New York. Elizabeth looked at the house, it looked like a palace. It also looked like Kings and Queens lived there. Her mother just laughed, "It's not that big," she said, "Yes it is!," replied Elizabeth. "May I paint my room? Do you think it will be ok?" "Yes!," said her mother, "You should see it first, but I need to help get the family settled. So you go in, and see what you think."
Elizabeth was so happy and not afraid. They lived in the back of the family's house. She went straight to her room. It was already painted pink and white, with a big bed, that had a top on it. It was so beautiful! She just stared. She went to look around the rest of the house. It had a beautiful kitchen, and looking in the bathroom, she realized what she had not seen before.

"Jesus! You were with me all along, even before I knew I needed You. You made the little room, and help me prepare it, knowing that I and my mom would need it. You have been guiding me every step of the way. You were listening to my prayers. The blessings, and protection, were with me without asking.

*The God of my strength, in whom I will trust; my shield
and the horn of my salvation,

my stronghold and my refuge; My Savior, You save me from violence.
2 Samuel 22:3 NKJV

"I love You Jesus! I'm so glad You came with us. I will always pray to You, for the rest of my life. Sometimes, it might be more than once a day."

Elizabeth always kept Jesus, close to her heart. One day, Elizabeth took the opportunity to ask her mother a question that had been troubling her. "Go ahead Elizabeth," said her mother. "Mom, how did Luc get into our house? Did you give him a key?" Her mother said, "No, dear. I would never have done that, but remember that lock on our front door, never, never worked right. So he must have been able to get in that way. But that is all behind us."

One year later, her mother met someone at Church. He was studying to be a Pastor. Elizabeth was now 12 years old. The Pastor could not believe how much she knew about the Bible. He always looked at her with kindness. Her mother said, **"Thank You, Jesus, for sending me someone special."**

*I have set the LORD always before me; because He is at my right hand I shall not be
moved. Psalm 16:8 NKJV

Chapter 7

Pastors

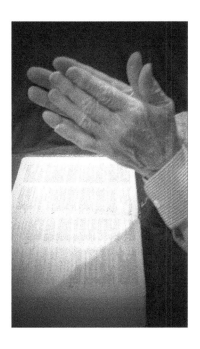

Pastors are just people, but are massagers of God's word. Jesus has picked them to help man, while on the path to God, they will finish the work. Pastors don't expect to be praised, or focused upon. For Christ is the goal, and our destiny. Pastors help man understand each passage in the Bible. Jesus has given Pastors what is needed to help man prepare for the day He returns.

He will walk with man once more, for when our judgement day comes. We don't have to complete the journey, but we must be on the path when Jesus returns, to lead us to the Father. We must carry, with us, hope, with a will to move forward, trust in the Father, and a soul reborn to Christ. Besides, a spirit that is connected to the Father, and a mind full of courage, that has no doubts.

Pastors are our gateway to the teachings of Christ. Remember, God will reveal when it's needed. Pastor's then help us understand the way to Jesus. We have to trust the Pastors, for they are like disciples of today's order. Jesus started the ministry, and the Pastors need to continue His work.

Pastors carry a lot of responsibilities, but these duties should not be over whelming. It is the highest rank under Jesus. A Pastor also spreads hope, spiritually to man, not just in Church. In a Pastors' travels, He also prepares a sermon of God's words, no matter who is in the congregation. A Pastor gives a lot, and has many titles.

Pastors are counsels, and assist, even in crisis situations. Remember, they are just people, not gods. Beside, having higher degrees of education, I feel the highest calling is faith. It is also spiritually connected to Christ, and the Holy Ghost. I know I've painted a picture of perfect person. I don't mean too. This is the path for a Pastor, and may God continue to bless them.

Pastors are an inspiration to man, and we must be open to God's words during their sermons. During the message of our Lord, Pastors are also leaders of their communities in today's time. Pastors teach, and we learn. Together, we tear down walls of evil. Pastors also give hope to the weak, so they can find their inner strength, as well of finding hope in Jesus. However, Pastors are not responsible, if your behavior takes a path to the left, and not stay on the right path.

Pastors deliver the word, and give you an ear, but you must walk your own path. When Pastors lead in worship, they give us strength to build up our will to succeed. Faith and hope makes the spirit soar, as well as finding fulfillment in the word. This is what, I think, Pastors are all about. We need to keep in mind, as Pastors help us find faith, they themselves must work to keep walking their own paths.

Pastors can't continue, without their own nourishment. I think Pastors also have to make sure to teach the words spoken by Christ. Pastors also realize, that in parting all of God's knowledge, is sometimes not an easy one. It can't be done by anyone, this job takes heart, and discipline in the word. I think of Pastors as innkeepers of the temple, keeping the will of God strong in His house.

Pastors always teach which side of the mountain to climb, as well as which river to drink from. Most of all, Pastors should never leave a man behind, without giving hope to all. God and Jesus give Pastors strength, and the word. Remember, Jesus, as does the Father speaks to all mankind, as well as guides us. Our Heavenly Father trusts the Pastors to be good leaders. It's not just through our Pastors God speaks, man must follow the word of God, even when the Pastors are not there. We have responsibilities as God's servants to be a free soul. Pastors move forward, rarely complaining. What lies inside, is the love for Christ. It is impossible to measure the love we have inside for Christ, because there is no measure.

When I sit in God's house, and listen to the message, there are times evil sticks his head out, and disguises himself with the hat of a Pastor. Because of our beliefs which are not necessarily the Pastor's, we firmly believe in Christs' words, no matter what. With love and trust, we see the reflection in the mirror. Evil can't hide from love, and because of our Pastor's teaching, we know what to look for in our daily walk.

We feel in our hearts and soul, Jesus' love. Keeping the connection with Christ, the seed of sin can't take root. Pastors carry burdens as man does, but the cloth of Christ keeps it from weighting them down. **Their steps are our cushions we float on the breath of God.**

Breathing in the freshness of the Holy Ghost, this is what my heart sees, and hears through Pastors. When Pastors share the word of God, I find hope to move forward. Don't take my love for my Pastor the wrong way, I only follow my God, and Him alone, will I bow my head too.

Thank You God for sending me Jesus, and thank You Jesus for saving my life. Please bless my Pastors, they are two great men and a woman of the cloth. For all mankind on earth, I wish them well, on the path that God has set them on, in life. Remember, keep faith, and belief in your heart with trust, and I hope you are blessed to be able to pick from the fruit of life. God's love and blessings gives mercy, and all wisdom will be revealed in your heart and soul. Your spirit will not only find peace, but connect, and forever walk with Jehvoah-Nissi.

*But the fruit of the Spirt is love, joy, peace, longsuffering, kindness, goodness,
faithfulness,
*gentleness, self-control. Against such there is no law. Galatians 5:22-23 NKJV

Chapter 8

The Shepard That Walked In Faith

Once upon a time, there was a Shepard that was poor, but rich in God. He always said his prayers, and praised God, while keeping good in his heart. He had a beautiful wife, very quiet, who was also very faithful in Christ. They had a son, just born. In a small village, the Shepard worked hard in the fields, only having enough to feed himself and his family.

There were times when taxes came due, if they could not pay, the collector took their women and children to do hard labor. After the Shepard paid his taxes, they would go hungry for days, because the collector took all they had. This year was going to be rough to start with, working day and night. The Shepard only had half of his tax money, and tax time was getting near.

The Shepard's prayer:

"Father in Heaven, is there any way to make up more in the fields, for the village people. So, we all may have enough to eat."

In prayer, the Shepard never asked for payment, but for work. **What would you have prayed for?** One day, just before taxes were due, the Shepard was working in the fields. He dropped to his knees, in prayer, and suddenly an idea came to him, but he also needed to talk to his wife. He told her, a journey was to begin on the seventh day. They needed to have faith.

The Shepard took two sheep, one donkey, food and clothes, and only his family. There would be no weapons on this journey, only a peaceful one, with faith in Christ and himself. This was also not to be a test, but a task. He felt Jesus needed him to spread the word of the Messiah's coming, and that he was to stay on the path. Always go right, there are no left turns.

The Shepard went to gather his supplies, and telling his wife about his plan. She saw the honor in this, but was concern for the safety of their son, and possibilities of danger. "Christ will provide," he said, "I have faith my wife, Christ will be all the protection we will need."

*There is no fear in love; but perfect love casts out fear, because fear involves torment.
But he who fears has not been made perfect in love. 1 John 4:18 NKJV

*"The LORD will fight for you, and you shall hold your peace." Exodus 14:14 NKJV

While the Shepard continued to pack, his wife went in, and kneeling by their son, she began to pray.

Her prayer:

"My Lord and Savior, I ask forgiveness for doubting You. I look to my faith in You, for guidance, and You have always blessed me and my family. I will forever be Your servant, and I will work hard on this journey, not just a support for my family, but as Your vessel.

*For we walk by faith, not by sight. 2 Corinthians 5:7 NKJV

His prayer:

"Thank You Lord, I'm looking to You for guidance. Faith in You carries trusts, and has no doubts. My soul believes, You know what's best for my family and me. I know You will protect us from the unknown, including charm that comes from evil. I will walk on steady feet, because You are my path."

He finished preparing for the journey, and after supper they rested. Then, on the morning of the seventh day, when he and his wife were preparing to leave, she noticed he didn't pack any weapons for hunting or fishing. He had one donkey and 2 sheep.

His words:

"I am confident, my wife, this is all we will need."

*And my God shall supply all your need according to His riches in glory by Christ Jesus.
Philippians 4:19 NKJV

People in the village had doubts regarding their survival. They started asking questions. How will you feed your family, and protect them without weapons against bandits, if attacked? The Shepard again expressed confidence for the journey, relying on God for their safety and success. The villagers responded that he should still take something for protection.

His words:

"I believe and trust in the Messiah. Our beliefs are strong and would have not been taken without our strong beliefs."

One man in the village said, "Take me and my family with you, and that way you will have weapons through me." This was a good friend of the Shepard. He put his hand on his shoulders and said, "My family and I are confident, and responsible for this journey. You, need to find your path to walk. I will pray for you."

*So then faith comes by hearing, and hearing by the word of God.
Romans 10:17 NKJV

The journey began. After 2 days of travel he walked beside his wife, who carried their son. Always at noon, they stop to rest. He had packed bread, fish, beef, fruits and vegetables, they would not be hungry. After resting and praying, he urged his wife to ride the donkey because there was a long walk ahead of them. When night came, they set up camp, and gave thanks before they ate their meal.

On another day, they would always rest until the first light, traveling to the right. One day, they came across a very small village. The Shepard shared with the villagers his believes in the coming of Christ, and telling them how the love of the Messiah can save them, and protect them from evil.

He also told them, how Christ, the Son of God, being the way to the Father, and how they should keep the faith. A day later, the Shepard and his wife continued their journey at first light. It was hot, but the clothes they were wearing covered their heads, and helped to shield them from the sun, while walking.

*The sun shall not strike you by day, nor the moon by might. Psalm 121:6 NKJV

***For the LORD God is a sun and shield; The LORD will give grace and glory; No good
thing will He withhold from those who walk uprightly. Psalm 84:11 NKJV**

Later, they came upon a river that they would need to cross. The Shepard studied the river, and looked to the heavens, for help.

***If any of you lacks wisdom, let him ask of God, who gives to all liberally and without
reproach, and it will be given to him. James 1:5 NKJV**

His idea was to make a long rope, long enough to reach the other side. He told his wife he would cross first. He used the rope to tie the sheep. Before he started to cross over, his wife expressed concern. He told her not to worry, for Jesus was crossing with him, and guiding him. The river seemed calm and a little deep, but appeared safe.

*GOD is our refuge and strength, a very present help in trouble. Psalm 46:1 NKJV

He made it to the other side, and tying the rope to a tree, he started back for his family. It was tiring work, but he made it back. However, his wife wanted him to rest. Still he needed to cross before night fall, so he put his wife and son on the donkeys back, telling her to hold on tight. Before crossing he said a prayer.

Half way across the river, the currents got stronger. Not expecting this, he slipped, and the donkey was pushed into the river. His wife called out to him, and turning to respond, he saw she had fallen from the donkey. His wife was trying to hold on with one hand, the baby tied to her, in a nap sack. Although weaken by the strong current, and his frequent trips across the river, he finally got to his wife and son, and cried out to Jesus.

His prayer:

"Jesus, give me the strength, I ask for mercy my Prince of Peace."

It took some work, but they finally made it to the other side. Holding each other tight, his wife soon realized their son was not breathing. Laying him down, he started to pray.

His prayer:
"In the name of Jesus, please give our son the light of life. Once more my Lord I ask You to please show our son mercy."

As the sun seemed too glow brighter, he turned his son upside down and miraculously heard a cry. His son began swing his arms, and his wife held him tight. She then gave thanks to their Lord and Savior. A gift of life was given. The Shepherd's faith and trust in Jesus grew stronger in that moment.

*Then Jesus spoke to them again, saying, "I am the light of the world. He who follows Me

shall not walk in darkness, but have the light of life." John
8:12 NKJV

Although he was tired and shaken, not wanting to leave his
family's side, he then went to take care of the animals. He
was happy to see the donkey survived, and on returning to his
family, he hugged his wife and son. He saw his wife drying
herself and their son, while, singing praises to the Messiah. As
he watched, he looked to the heavens.

His words:

"I realize we have no reason to doubt all the miracles You
have bless us with. I have no right to doubt, my Lord. I'm
just weary, but my spirit knows You're there for us. I need
to pray to restore my strength. Even if I was blind, You
would be worth the journey, my Lord Christ. Will You
give me a sign, that I'm doing the right thing and going the
right way?"

Hard work, with faith, can lead to the great things.

*In all labor there is profit, but idle chatter leads only to
poverty.
Proverbs 14:23 NKJV

After praying together, and setting up camp, they rested so they
could start early at first light. Waking up, he knew he would
have to find food and water. The river took what water and food
they had. He would also have to make something to carry water
in, for the rest of the journey.
The Shepard looked to the heavens. Jesus will find a way. He
made a fishing net with part of his robe, and used a portion of

a tree truck to form a cup. While fishing, he noticed the river was calmer. It puzzled him. Could it have been evil trying to block him from Jesus, and spreading the word?

His words:

"I will not lose my faith in Jesus, and I will not be turned around."

The family had fish and water before starting their journey again. By noon, they came up on another village, stopping to rest, and trade for supplies. While there, they told their story of why they were on the journey, partially the coming of the Messiah. The Shepard told them about faith, and he told them what happened at the river, and how Jesus blessed them and saved their son.
Some agreed, it was a blessing and a miracle. Others, unbelievers, said, it was luck. Why would you do this to your family? The Shepard looked to the heavens for inspiration. He began to tell the doubting villagers the story of Jesus, and said, that Jesus loved him, and his family, and walks with them.

His words:

"Do you not care He sacrificed Himself for you."

Not many listened, or cared, but those who did, prayed with him and his wife. The unbelievers still thought it was unwise to put his family at risk.

*Wait on the Lord; be of good courage, and He shall strengthen your heart; Wait, I say, on the LORD! Psalm 27:14 NKJV

When night fell, they rested in a stable, belonging to believers. At first light, he realized someone had stolen their sheep. No one saw a thing, and sad, nothing could be done. The Shepard and his wife packed their supplies, and started their journey with only a donkey. The trek would be long, and the unbelievers who took the sheep, just laugh. "How is your faith now, Shepard?," they asked. They were surprise to find the Shepard in good spirits, ready to leave.

The Shepard said a prayer. It was noon, and time to rest. Setting up camp, they ate some bread and fish. His wife was worried, "What will we do without the sheep to pay for food?" "Jesus will make a way." replied the Shepard. Then bowing their heads, they prayed in silence.

Her prayer:

"Lord, I don't wish to lose faith, but please show me a sign, thou are still with us. You have shown us a great miracle, but today we need just a sign of loving comfort."

His prayer:

"I can feel You in my Heart and soul. I cast my burdens and worries on You. Lord, I ask if You can give us some comfort in our spirt."

How can this be, two people praying in silence, and asking for the same thing. They never asked God to make it easy, just to stay with them, as they met all challenges.

After resting, they began their journey again. Just before dark, they came to a junction in the path. There was nothing to tell them which way to go. From a grove of trees, a woman appeared, informing them, bandits has just come, and gone to the right.

The Shepard thanked her, but said, "We must stay on the path, and it only goes right." "We must go left." said his wife. The Shepard laid hands on his wife's shoulders.

His words:

"When on the path stay to the right, we must have faith."

After praying silently, the wife found her strength and courage, and love for Christ. So, they went right.

Down the road, they came upon ten men, blocking the path. Their leader said, "This is our road, and you must pay to be granted passage!" The Shepard explains they were poor, and only had a donkey. The men just laughed at them. The leader said, "If you have no gold or coins, than give us your wife and the donkey, and you may pass with your son."

The Shepard told them the story of why they were on the journey, and informing them of the coming of Christ, hoping for mercy. It did nothing to soften the bandits' hearts. So, the Shepard and his wife got to their knees, and bowing their heads, began to pray out loud.

Their prayer:

*The Lord is my shepherd; I shall not want.
*He makes me to lie down in green pastures; He leads me beside the still waters.
*He restores my soul; He leads me in the paths of righteousness for His name's sake.
*Yea, though I walk through the valley of the shadow of death, I will fear no evil; For You

are with me; Your rod and Your staff, they comfort me.
*You prepare a table before me in the presence of my enemies; You anoint my head with
oil; my cup runs over.
*Surely goodness and mercy shall follow me all the days of my life; And I will dwell in the
house of the LORD forever. Psalm 23:1-6 NKJV

While the Shepard and his wife were praying, the leader and his men grow impatient. The leader told his men to get the wife and the donkey, even thou the Shepard was looking to the heavens for mercy.

*I WILL lift up my eyes to the hills--from whence comes my help?
*My help comes from the LORD, who made heaven and earth. Psalm 121:1-2 NKJV

*Behold, He who keeps Israel shall neither slumber nor sleep. Psalm 121:4 NKJV

As the men approached the wife, who was still on her knees holding their son, something miraculous happen. Their son, who had turned six months old, looked at the men, smiled, waved his arms, and suddenly, everything, became quiet. Only the baby could be heard. Something, then happen to the men's hearts. Although it was just baby talk, it melted their hearts.
The leader said, "I will let you all pass, but only if I can hold the child just once." The Shepard, looking surprised, and a little confused, agreed to all the men holding the child. The leader kept his promise, and let them all pass.
The Shepard and his family proceeded, but it was becoming dark, and it was time to rest. They sat watching, their gift from

God, sleeping peacefully. Everything had a purpose, and would be a help on the journey.

While they slept, the Shepard dreamed of abundant crops, plenty of water, which would make everyone happy. When they awoke, the Shepard told his wife of the dream. He said, "I think we're home."

Her words:

"Where is home?"

His words:

"Here!"

She looked around, and seeing no trees or water, still knew God would provide. The Shepard went to see if he could find food and water. Walking to the edge of the camp, he stopped, and stared. His wife, growing alarmed, asked, "What's wrong?"

Getting no answer, she went to his side, and she too just stared. They could not believe their eyes. Before them was a clearing, as far as the eyes could see, full of fruit trees, a river, with miles and miles of grass, and five sheep. It was everything needed to start a new life. This was not only comfort, but a blessing.

All their prayers to God have always been heard. God has also always provided, and given protection. It was an even greater blessing, because the Shepard and his family had found themselves back at the village where they had started.

When awaken, what lay before them, was a field full of crop, enough to pay taxes, and feed their families. Everyone remembered the Shepard, who on his knees, prayed over the villagers, before leaving on his journey. The Shepard held his wife and son, and spoke.

His words:

"Our trust in Jesus kept us safe. Our faith in Him guided us home. His pure soul was our eyes, and keeping our spirit in Christ, gave us a feeling of peace. The riches of God lay before us. My wife, sometimes your blinded faith will guide you through, but your trust in the unknown is not wrong. If you seek Jesus, you may not see, but your soul feels the comfort of the calming love from heaven. Your spirit stands strong and unshaken. Why is that? I say, it's because God sent Jesus, and Jesus gave man the tools that can carry great weight."

Use the strength He gave you, and go forward with the courage, as the Shepard and his wife did, you just need to believe, truly believe. The tools are yours to have, unless you give freely. Besides, a mind to think with, and words from the Bible, and a heart to love. With God in mind, you can trust someone, even if something is not seen.

Believe in one's self, faith in the Father, who never leaves our side, and a soul with unlimited power. Under Christ, remember there's power in prayer, hope that gives you the will, and with the will, comes courage. Move forward to victory. A Shepard's dream came true under Christ.

*Now may the God of hope fill you with all joy and peace in believing, that you may
abound in hope by the power of the Holy Spirit. Romans 15:13 NKJV

Sometimes, you just have to have faith, and believe
in hope. Dreams are good for man, under **<u>GOD.</u>**

Chapter 9

The Meaning Of Christ Our Savior's Name

I listen to a song today, and it inspired me to write all the names used, and find their meaning. I could not believe what I found. I know, in my heart, it would be wonderful, so uplifting to my soul and spirit. Remember, I'm finding my way back. So, I wish to know all the knowledge God will reveal, but first I must find my path.

Here is my list:

Jehovah - - is Hebrew for God or The Lord. It is said that **Jehovah** is used to reveal God as a truly supreme or eternal.

*And God said to Moses, "I AM WHO I AM." And He said, "Thus you shall say to the children of Israel, "I AM has sent me to you."' Exodus 3:14 NKJV

I read that the Name, **Nissi**, used in the Bible, means-**Jehovah-Nissi**. It is also Hebrew and was given to by Moses for the altar, which he built to celebrate the defeat of the Amalekites at Rephidim.

Jehovah-Nissi - - also means the Lord is our banner.

Jehovah-Shalom - - this is used, and means peace, and it can also mean peace from the Lord.

Jehovah-Jireh - - book of Genesis.

Jehovah-Jireh or **Yahweh Yireh - -** is the same name. It was a place in Moriah, a place and time of Abraham.

Jehovah-Jireh - - means a provider.

*And Abraham called the name of the place, The-LORD-Will-Provide; as it is said to this day, "In the Mount of the LORD it shall be provided." Genesis 22:14 NKJV

Some worshipers, I heard, use **Divine** when speaking of Jesus.

Divine - - means to forgive those who make mistakes, to try to live in God's will.

Jesus is known for His ministry, but Jesus, the **Anoint One**, was predicted in the Bible.

*But while he thought about these things, behold, an angel of the Lord appeared to him in
a dream, saying, "Joseph, son of David, do not be afraid to take to you Mary your wife,
for that which is conceived in her is of the Holy Spirit.
* "And she will bring forth a Son, and you shall call his name Jesus, for He will save His
people from their sins." Matthew 1:20-21 NKJV

Messiah - - means **Anointed One** the birth of Jesus the Messiah.

* *"Behold, the virgin shall be with child, and bear a Son, and they shall call* His *name*

Im-man-u-el," which is translated, "God with us." Matthew 1:23 NKJV

*For unto us a Child is born, unto us a Son is given; and the government will be upon His
shoulder. And His name will be called Wonderful, Counselor, Mighty God, Everlasting
Father, Prince of Peace. Isaiah 9:6 NKJV

*Simon Peter answered and said, "You are the Christ, the Son of the living God."
Matthew 16:16 NKJV

When reading the names, we should know their meaning, and understand why we need them. These names are important, because they stand for God and the Son. When you hear them out loud, you should know who they are.

*And daily in the temple, and in every house, they did not cease teaching and preaching
Jesus as the Christ. Acts 5:42 NKJV

We owe so much to Jesus for coming, and putting Himself in the path of the words of hatred for us, and putting Himself in front of the stones thrown from evil. He also put himself in the path of the 30 lashes, for taking a crown meant for pain and humiliation, also for taking 3 nails meant to cause sorrow and suffering.
He also sacrificed Himself on a symbol that should be used for prayer, but was used to cause misery and begging for mercy before death. Jesus, being the Messiah, gave forgiveness, and for told man's distraction. We thank Jesus for looking to the heavens, and asking forgiveness from the Father. In addition, for mankind, even those who don't know why they hate, Jesus loves.

Chapter 10

The Wisdom Of God

*For the LORD gives wisdom; from His mouth come knowledge and understanding;
Proverbs 2:6 NKJV

Having wisdom from God, is the highest blessing given. It makes you feel humble that God, the Creator, and Author, thought we were worthy of this wisdom. I see more and more, as the knowledge of God's wisdom is revealed. This wisdom lets us see God's guidance, and know what works we are expected to do day by day.

Wisdom is so we, the followers, know good from bad, and pray with praise to our God. We joyfully sing a song to be heard around the world. Wisdom also brings us together, under one roof, for under God, we are family. God sees not the body of man, but his spirit. It also lies in the heart, is righteousness and of love.

Remember, wisdom also shows you how to look pass the wrongs, and find the good that was there before. Through the wisdom of God, and the ministry of Jesus, we learn to forgive. We also give mercy as Christ does, that's love.

*Happy is the man who finds wisdom, and the man who gains understanding;
*For her proceeds are better than the profits of silver, and her gain than fine gold.
Proverbs 3:13-14 NKJV

Wisdom is solid ground, for God, will not let our feet slip off the path as long as, we live in the word of Christ. Keep in mind, if you slip, it is not God who let go, but you. Wisdom is many things, but only the wisdom from God will help, while working your way back to the Kingdom. Only the wisdom from the Holy Bible has the key to the knowledge, and when we speak, it is the wisdom of God's words. We speak of the coming of our Lord. I have no illusions that this will be easy, just because I have the wisdom, because sin is always out there. Sin is always watching and waiting, so I must stand guard. I pray day and night for my heart, soul, spirit, and faith. We also keep God's words, so sin does not slip into our lives.

We need to understand the law and commandments of the Bible, its righteousness and good for the author, God. We need wisdom to see the story God has written, and keep it close to our heart, for there can be nothing greater.

*Trust in the Lord with all your heart, and lean not on your own understanding;
*In all your ways acknowledge Him, and He shall direct your paths.
Proverbs 3:5-6 NKJV

Wisdom gives strength to rise, and the will to run the race. God makes sure we beat sin by a mile. Wisdom makes you strong. We fight with the weapon God gave us, the flag of peace and love.

Wisdom helps our faith, look pass the mistakes, and learn from them so, we can become pure in His name. Wisdom leaves us hope for tomorrow, and watches the sun rise. Wisdom is the belief in Christ, and confidence in one's self. We believe He is the Almighty God, nothing less or more. Wisdom is unshaken, no matter the temptation or uneven ground.

Wisdom is also the Almighty Holy Ghost, giving Spiritual comfort, and sets our mind free. So, I tell you, don't be of greed, it will only bring weariness and pain. Your days will sometimes be cloudy. We must keep the wisdom of God at the forefront, and away from greed.

Sometimes, man thinks he is wiser, and knows all, because of the fortune he has built. He lets this rule his heart and soul. Don't be consumed by sin. I want to encourage you to read, and receive the riches God gives with the wisdom of knowledge.

*Happy is the man who finds wisdom, and the man who gains understanding;
*For her proceeds are better than the profits of silver, and her gain than fine gold.
*She is more precious than rubies, and all the things you may desire cannot compare with
her.
*Length of days is in her right hand, in her left hand riches and honor.
*Her ways are ways of pleasantness, and all her paths are peace.
*She is a tree of life to those who take hold of her, and happy are all who retain her.
Proverbs 3:13-18 NKJV

God's wisdom is so precious, you can't compare it to gold or silver. It can also show you long life. Once you have the wisdom, make sure you understand what you have in your life. Having wisdom, you must continue to study and learn. So, you can receive it daily.

There is an **<u>Oasis of Peace - - The Tree of Life.</u>** It isn't for him or her, but all mankind. Using rubies, gold and silver is to let you see the value of God's wisdom. Yes, rubies are priceless, but if you had the valve of God's wisdom, it is ever lasting.

Chapter 11

It's Been A Life Time, It Seems

It has been a life time since I heard the birds sing, and the **whispers of the warm welcome of life and love.** I sometimes dream of a trip up the mountain, climbing to the top. I imagine **whispers of encouragement** to not give up, and keep faith. I love the **gentle hugs to the heart from heaven**, especially when the pain and hurt comes. Most of all, I miss the connections to Christ. I wish for Him to forgive, and show mercy. Jesus is someone I can call on not just when **the storm knocks at the door.**

Jesus is the one I can call on to listen, even when it's just **chatting about nothing,** as if I was **William Shakespeare.** I just found the saying about looking for hope and riches everywhere. Well, it can't be found unless you look to the mountain called **Mount Sinai.** I know now, and can see, that Jesus is the key. I wish to testify in open court, keeping nothing from my Lord. With a true heart, there are times I look to the heavens, and feel sorrow, that I wasted time missing out on the love of Christ. Searching for something only Jesus can give, I shed a tear, not from weariness, but because of the beauty of Jesus. I wonder how I got to be so worthy of His love?

That to me, shows deep love, He and the Father have for mankind. I have found my faith and belief in Christ. I thought, at one time, it was lost. I shell move forward with the spirit, both with love for Christ. When my heart is fully open, I began to feel the cloth of Jesus' protection. Yes, I'm climbing the mountain, not for the riches, but for the love and mercy, with compassion, only the Father and Son can give.

At the mountain top, I look across as far as my eyes can see. Instead of looking through eyes of man, I look through my heart, and love for Jesus. Christ's guidance shows me what the Kingdom and the Garden would have look like. The new Garden will be once more, when the **trumpets of victory ring out like, gospel music.**

*Seek the LORD while He may be found, call upon Him while He is near.
*Let the wicked forsake his way, and the unrighteous man his thoughts; Let him return to
the LORD, and He will have mercy on him; and to our God, for He will abundantly
pardon. Isaiah 55:6-7 NKJV

It's been a long time, and today, I realize that I have not felt, this love. I haven't stepped in yet, and what I mean by that, is I've not let myself believe and I have not trusted. Deep down, I was holding back, and just that, can stop any real connection to Christ. I realized I had to open my heart, but did you know I needed to open my mind as well?
All along, the answer was always there. As it's written, I needed to find my path and be willing to walk it. I also needed to meet all challenges that come with the beliefs. Christ is with me, so I can receive blessings. Let me say, Christ does not hold back on blessings. You must know, if part of your mind is closed off to them.

Christ does not wish you to have half a blessing, but a whole. When we walk in the name of the Holy Ghost, it is **cushioned by the cloth of Christ**. I look upon the Heavenly Father and Son as a team. One, who guides to the Father and the Father who gives forgiveness, and mercy together shining, the light on the path. So, we may see a head, and have no confusion.

It's been a long time, but my path is here. I will not waste my gift of forgiveness and mercy, by keeping love for this earth, and its love of emptiness, or the love of the flesh. I found it only leads to sin, and I will not let pride control my destiny. These things can block my path, it seems, but I will not stand in the pool of nothing with empty promises.

I compare this to the **ocean with soft waves,** where Christ stood, waving a hand to **calm the storm.** Here, you can swim in blessings. I ask you, after reading this, has it been like a life time for you? If so, stop and open your heart, and look to the mountain. When you find the steps, climb with hope and trust, but most of all, with the love for Christ.

*And let the peace of God rule in your hearts, to which also you were called in one body;
and be thankful. Colossians 3:15 NKJV

<u>Don't Let A Life Time Pass You By!</u>

Chapter 12

The Circle Of Life

Life should always bring you joy, and compassion filling you. Your soul must always know where to go, and most of all, you should trust the journey. Your strength should never leave you, for at every turn, you have nourishment to feed you. We always need to feed our spirit, soul, and mind.

Torches should light up the darkness for you, and you should always be able to see where you're going. Don't mistakenly let the "**Fragrance**" of rose's beckon you. The fragrance will filter out any unpleasantness that arises. You should not go through life with ignorance of your surroundings.

You should receive all the knowledge that life offers, and not let weaknesses be an excuse to quit. Everything about you is not weak. We must find that inner strength, and use it, and pull ourselves up. Don't get bitter, because it's taking too long. In the end, it only means, it's going to be greater. So, chose wisely!

Choices and chances you take are life changers. Take your time, and don't be afraid to ask questions, or for directions. The person that asks questions is smarter than a genius, because he did not let his pride get in the way of his success of finding Jesus.

When you made a mistake, you were still so much bigger than most, because you stood up with head held high, with your shoulders back. You say out loud, "Clearly, it was me" and absorbed your punishment with grace. Who does that? That's someone full of Christ, and so brave. God was watching, not the man, but his heart. We are excepting help, and showing gratitude instead of envy and jealousy.

"Jesus," You are the one who taught me, that from the depth of Your heart, You went and sacrifice everything for others, not thinking of Yourself first. You also never showed disappointment, or indifference. This is the gift I have been blessed with, thanks for the **nudge**. Several times, I forgot to move quickly. When I look up to heaven, I see love and kindness there.

The nudge is never hard, but tender. It gets me going. I know we are judged by our work, but mostly, how we love. Thank You Jesus, for having faith in me. I'm trusting You will be there, should I fall. If I do, I trust You will catch me with loving arms. Love can set souls and spirits free, including darkness in the day, and bring them into the light. The sun warms mu heart. "**Thank You** for helping me find my way back to God."

I have surrounded all. With praise and prayer, we can find the step and journey to the Kingdom. So, I kneel down. Why, because I've learned, to walk with You. I'll pray and give praise and honor to Jesus, for making it possible for me to find my treasure. It was here all along—life vs the treasure.

**Thank You God for sending me Jesus and
thank You Jesus for saving my life.**

AMEN!

Chapter 13

Mirror Of The Bible

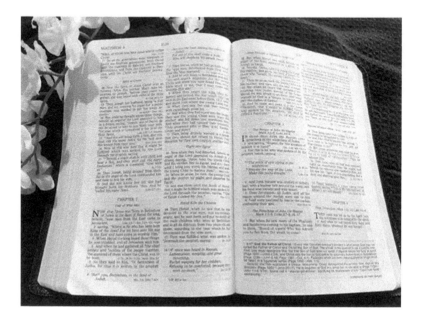

I read somewhere that the Bible is like a mirror. I'm thinking about how that would look? This is what I came up with. When you open your Bible and start to read, you'll see through Christ's words. The mirror is a reflection of yourself. It shows all the things man needs to repent for, and ask God's forgiveness and mercy. As you read the Bible, a mirror also shows the pain and sorrow on your shoulders, and you see the reflection of the path. You must take the path through Jesus to the Father, not an easy path, but one that's not impossible with Christ.

This mirror, in the Bible, is a reflection of God and His love for mankind. It also shows the beauty and love, which gives hope. It also leads to faith, with this, your heart fills with strong words. God also connects to the soul and spirit. You know God's love, but you must open the Bible first and believe. In the words spoken by our Lord, when you follow these commandments, any weariness or weakness falls in the sea.

There are no limits to forgiveness, and the blessings that follow. Remember, all praise and thanks, go to our Lord Christ. We are rewarded for a job well done. So, you see, you are not without the riches of life, holding, silver and gold in your hands. Riches never hold promises. Looking in the mirror of the Bible, shows them melting away, but the riches of Christ holds strong with hope. Looking in the Bible, it also shows evil no longer holds court here. The bondage of evil, held over man, is being destroyed by love and peace, a weapon of power, given by Christ.

***If then you were raised with Christ, seek those things which are above, where Christ is,
sitting at the right hand of God. Colossians 3:1 NKJV**

This mirror reflects spiritual guidance from Christ. Yes, love takes it's time, not rushing you, and love never covets you.

**Love does not walk on your miss fortune.
Love is faithful and loyal.
Love has no pride that guides.
Love is kind, so you can't' provoke it.
Love rejoices in the words of Christ.
Love carries righteousness, but never is unrighteous.
Love stands strong, and you can lean on it.
Love won't fail you.
Love holds up thy neighbors.
Love endures, so you don't suffer, and comes up the victor.**

**Love covers you from evil, that comes in the form of a storm.
Love carries the burdens for you.
Love has no fear, because it is written, that if you fear, you
have no love.**

This is what the mirror of the Bible shows me, and I only see
the reflection of Christ. We must protect our right to be on the
path. Jesus leads, and when we repent, it finds the connection
to God through Jesus. When evil is before us, we can remember
what the reflection of the mirror is all about.

<u>Love, Hope, Faith, Belief, Trust, in God,
and in His love for mankind.</u>

Jesus has walked with man, teaching and guiding to the right
path, which is the promise of everlasting life in God's Kingdom.
Walking to the left, were evil is the guide, and is one of only
sorrow and pain and sadness. When storms come, evil leaves
you without an umbrella. The storm also leaves you with empty
promises, standing guard at every turn. There is no everlasting
life, no rest only death.

The wrong path weights you down with every step, making you
believe there's a cliff. There is no hope of crossing, and if you
fall, you are trampled without mercy. This is what you are left
with, without the reflection of the Bible's mirror.

There are no promises to the left, just hidden lies in the dark.
Evil is loyal to no one but himself. As you can see, when
you open the Bible, and look in the mirror, there are blessings
beyond measure, and nothing is without victory. In this mirror,
you are washed in the blood of Jesus. We are spiritually reborn
to Christ, once more leaving man's world behind.

* "Behold, I stand at the door and knock. If anyone hears My voice and opens the door, I
will come in to him and dine with him, and he with Me. Revelation 3:20 NKJV

I believe, even though you walk the earth, the reflection shows you walking in an outer garden of the Kingdom. What you also see is hope, and love without burdens weighing you down. Man on earth can't promise anything. They just can't give. What's needed it's not within their power, but with Jesus guiding us to the Father, when you ask for forgiveness and mercy, nothing is impossible for our Lord Christ. You only need to callout His name with a true heart, and behold, He stands before you in the mirror of the Bible with open arms.

* "If My people who are called by My name will humble themselves, and pray and seek
My face, and turn from their wicked ways, then I will hear from heaven, and will
forgive their sin and heal their land. 2 Chronicles 7:14 NKJV

Chapter 14

Jesus Always Finds A Way

Jesus is always there for us, faith finds a way even when you weren't sure. You question your faith. Even when you doubt it, faith always prevails. When you took a stand, and the ground violently shook, Jesus appeared in our minds. Everything stood still, because faith finds a way.

When you began to walk, and it looked as if you were falling behind, you might look around, not sure which way to turn. Confusion may set in, and Jesus lets you know He is beside you. Keeping pace right than, you realize faith finds a way.

When the road appears before you, your soul knows, this is the start of the journey home. The road also takes you up hill, and you must climb to finish your journey. It's not an easy task, but you bare it anyway.

The road may even out, but it's still rough, but you push on because every step you take, **Jesus takes two steps with you, clearing the path**. He encourages you not to give up, keeping in mind, Jesus has not left you to bare it alone. He is always two steps ahead, with guidance and **the candle light of Christ**. He provides protection, giving you added strength.

The road includes all your hopes and dreams. There is also difficulty, but all the trials you come across and conquered, will not stop the path you are walking in Christ. God and Jesus are fighting this battle for you. They will lose nothing, if you don't wish to fight against evil. If you don't follow, you lose life and peace.

* "Therefore be merciful, just as your Father also is merciful. Luke 6:36 NKJV

Don't you feel the love and blessings raining down from heaven? 'It's because of all the love the Father has for you. It flows through God, to the Son, to us. Again, faith finds a way. We also must put on God's armor for the battle. When putting on the armor, you need to pledge loyalty to His love, and bring faith without doubt. He is the Almighty God. Again, faith finds a way.

If it is in your heart, Jesus always finds a way. Jesus keeps his promises, but you must work hard. Keep praying for opens doors. Worship, and receive Jesus in our heart and soul. So, we may save our spirits from darkness.

*For **"He who would love life and see good days, let him refrain his tongue from evil, and**
his lips from speaking deceit.
*Let him turn away from evil and do good; let him seek **peace and pursue it.**
*For the eyes of the LORD are on the righteous, and His **ears are open to their prayers;**
but the face of the LORD is against those who do evil," 1 Peter 3:10-12 NKJV

Chapter 15

Peace Is A Given

I will work for peace, offing encouragement and guidance. I will try and encourage love and hope with my neighbors. For the sick and injured, I will lay hands, and pray for healing. I will leave doubt behind, and trust my faith in Jesus. I will not worry about things that have no meaning, and look to Jesus for what I can't control. I bow down before the Holy Ghost.

I will not give up hope, so others can draw on it, through darkness. When other's over take me, I will use my faith to light my way. I will not take the road of sadness, but the route to joy, and sing out loud praises. I have complete faith in Jesus, and will do His will.

I will lend an ear, and understanding, with compassion, on my journey, for those in need of me. I will receive Jesus' unconditional love in my giving to others, because I do so from the heart, not for profit. I choose to turn Lucifer's negative words to positive words of love.

*** "He who believes in the Son has everlasting life; and he who does not believe the Son
shall not see life, but the wrath of God abides on him." John 3:36 NKJV**

Jesus will give pardon in all things. We must keep faith, because all will be revealed to us in the Kingdom of life. When we are pardon, and washed in the blessed water of the Holy Spirit, we will be reborn and given eternal life. Let us be the instrument of Jesus, and spread the word of the coming of Christ.

Don't let evil put seeds of lies in your mind. Never be blocked from Jesus, because the road of evil doesn't want you to go on your journey that leads to heaven. Always look to heaven for guidance, if confused. When the ship sails across the sea to Holiness, we the believers, will be the passengers. Remember the words that have been spoken.

> **The way to the Father is through Jesus. We move forward, and walk the path to glory, remember the saying, "It's better to give than to receive, to share a blessing that is much better."**

*But I will sing of Your power; Yes, I will sing aloud of Your mercy in the morning; for
You have been my defense and refuge in the day of my trouble.
Psalm 59:16 NKJV

In the eye of Jesus, He did not want anyone left behind. This was His way of loving us, with salvation given to man. So, I walk in the path, given love to those I pass on my journey.

*Brethren, I do not count myself to have apprehended; but one thing I do, forgetting those
things which are behind and reaching forward to those things which are ahead.
*I press toward the goal for the prize of the upward call of God in Christ Jesus.
Philippians 3:13-14 NKJV

Chapter 16

A Positive Word For You

I stand before you, because God has blessed me with life. Look at me, because you can see I'm here due to His mercy. I'm also living the word. I've also pass trouble, that evil put before me. The pain was lifted with one word—**Jehovah**. All my hate is gone, thanks to my Lord **Nissi**, and the sadness is dissolved by **Jehovah-Shalom**.

The world is a happier place, for God has sent a Savior. The hated laughter directed at me, will never be heard again, nothing can make me fall, for the cross shines bright on my path. Now, I can see the cracks, and I will not stumble. So, you see, I stand tall. When the water rises, and the earth shakes, I think of **Jehovan-Jirch**, and I'm provided with helping hands. When I cross the water, everything begins to settle down. I hold my head up high, proud of being blessed with love. My faith is strong with the helping of Almighty God.

I can't be moved or turn around, not by man, or beast. I'm here, with the will to hope and dream. Again, evil can't crush me. My path is for Jesus, and I'm protected. I have the belief in the Anoint One, and will embrace His love, and follow His commands where ever they lead.

Others will not let me decide how I love. **I will live in the word!** I stand, without shame, of who my Lord says I am. I'm here with love and compassion in my heart. I have a positive attitude, and my mind is clear. There will be no negative thoughts, or doubts in this body. My will is strong, for it feeds off my spirit. It gets its nourishment from the Holy Ghost. I will approach everything with God on my mind, I walk with **Jehovah-Nissi.** As of flag of peace and shield, so when you see me, I'm not standing alone.

***If someone says, "I love God," and hates his brother, he is a liar; for he who does not
love his brother whom he has seen, how can he love God whom he has not seen?
1 John 4:20 NKJV**

I don't stand taller than the Messiah, but I still have love, and strength due to Him. However, I do stand taller than evil, for I have Christ holding me up. I stand before you, saying, **"Look at me, I'm living the word!"** I also stand here today because Jesus thought I was worthy, and loved me. He stood in front of me, facing evil that controlled man.

He took my lashes for me, and withstood foul language. He never was a coward from the stones being thrown at Him. This is what Jesus, the Messiah, took standing in my place. He carried the cross Himself, which should be a symbol of love and peace. However, in reality, it was to be His stake to be crucified. Even though Jesus knew this was coming, He never weakened, or asked for mercy.

Despite the sins of man, Jesus stood strong for me. I'm so glad He though so much of me. I stand here today, knowing Jesus was to be sacrifice for me, so I may love. Jesus took every nail for all our sins. It gave forgiveness, and others a **"Garden of Love."** I call it **"Holy Ground."** That is where we began before, and will start over. Only stronger, and have more knowledge. I've read, while on the cross, legs were broken, but God protected Jesus' legs from harm. Today, I stand on the legs given by Christ, our Lord.

***Believe Me that I am in the Father and the Father in Me, or else believe Me for the sake
of the works themselves. John 14:11 NKJV**

I also stand with love and faith, believing that the Holy Spirt will surround me, so I will be safe knowing of all of Jesus' sacrifices. I stand before, entirely whole, from within. I give praise to the Messiah! The **Jehovah-Shalom ... peace from my Lord, thank You Jesus.**

***You will show me the path of life; In Your presence is fullness of joy; At Your right hand
are pleasures forevermore. Psalm 16:11 NKJV**

*Rejoice in the LORD always. Again I will say, rejoice! Philippians 4:4 NKJV

Have you also noticed that everything is always to the right of God? This is what started me saying, **the path is always to the right**. I hope you find peace, not just of mind, but spiritual.

Be blessed in all you've done, and will do.

God Be With You All

Chapter 17

I Like To Believe

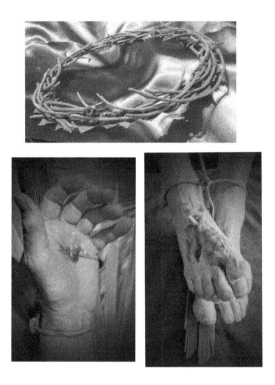

I would like to believe the nails used on Jesus and His head piece were representative of something.

*Then Jesus said, "Father, forgive them, for they do not know what they do." And they
divided His garments and cast lots. Luke 23:34 NKJV

His head piece, instead of pain, really showed him to be King, the Anointed One. Besides, the nail in His right hand represented the life of man, and a chance to repent and receive redemption. The nail in His left hand represented shame, for leaving the path of God. Besides the sin, mankind still had a choice to save himself, and receive salvation. The nails in His feet represented peace and love.

Jesus had strong faith in who He was, the Son of God, and to kneel before Him with trust and faith. When man kneels before Jesus, and sees Him on the cross, he looks into Jesus' eyes. He imagines it's just like being home. Jesus sacrificed His life for mankind. When we let Him down, we can still return to the path. **Just believe!** Let's give praise, and thank Him for life. When Jesus was crucified, He received lashes. No one knows how many, but I would like to believe it was seven. This is what it meant for man:

Lash number one- -
The spirit of man, gaining strength to stand, and find his way back to the path of God.
Lash number two - -
The soul of man, reaching for Christ.
Lash number three - -
Faith in the Son, that He will walk with man once more.
Lash number four - -
Trusting once again, that His love is what we need to be whole again.
Lash number five - -
Finding peace in the word of God.
Lash number six - -
Believe that man can rise, and ask forgiveness from the Father.
Lash number seven - -
Knowing there is hope for mankind, because God said, we are worthy, and sent His Son to save man.

When they pierced Jesus Christ on the right side, the water flowing from the wound, was pure. It cleansed man, and the blood that flowed, gave blessings and new life. It also opened doors for mankind. **We** must **repent!** I say this to those who don't believe that Jesus only spoke kind words, and love with healing hands. As Jesus traveled, He healed the sick, and helped the blind to see. In my Journey, I believe this is what the head piece and nails stood for.

In offering peace for the soul, I say, only someone of Christ would give that, and have a pure heart. This is where man can let his mind wonder, and have a chance to give a good word. Don't all words spoken by Jesus come true? Jesus never spoke of anything that He would not give man.

He chose not to see man hungry, or homeless. Besides, a woman, who needing shelter, loving care, and protection from evil. He also wanted to protect a child in the same way. This includes saving them from the man, who chooses to help, but only for profit, and never cares.

*Do not be overcome by evil, but overcome evil with good. Romans 12:21 NKJV

Remember, we are judged, not by those who refuse help, but by what we give and our acts. You need to know this, God sits with the weak and helpless, watching, as you pass by.

*Let every soul be subject to the governing authorities. For there is no authority except
from God, and the authorities that exist are appointed by God. Romans 13:1 NKJV

We have the power that Jesus gave us to lift our brothers and sisters up, and give hope. Jesus gave man eyes to see the child, and shelter them, and stop the cycle. We have the power to nourish them, and those who turn from His love, need our prayers, too. Just don't give up.

I believe showing love, and teaching the word, is the man's job to stop Satan. God gave us the tools, and sending Jesus to guide man to the path. We must not let Satan have them, or their souls. We must fight with peace.

*Therefore *"If your enemy is hungry, feed him; If he is thirsty, give him a drink; For in so*
doing you will heap coals of fire on his head." **Romans 12:20 NKJV**

We don't have to be god's to cast evil from our lives. We can face evil, and say, **be gone,** and call out for Jesus. We must get back on the path, and show our children what is right, and teach them of His love. We must show, through love, so they understand God, and why Jesus scarified Himself. In doing this, we become stronger. In doing this, with strength in faith, Satan can't defeat us.

I heard a song, "There Is Power," written by Lincoln Brewster, whose lyrics go something like this ...

There is power
In the name of Jesus.
There is power
Power in His name ...

So, if His name carries that much power, can you imagine what His words can do?

*not returning evil for evil or reviling for reviling, but on the contrary blessing, knowing
that you were called to this, that you may inherit a blessing.
1 Peter 3:9 NKJV

So take with you today, and keep in mind, when you see someone, don't let them draw you in, but fight with love. There's always a verse to help you. Keep your Bible close, study it, and don't let it get dusty. We must reset our mind, and connect with Christ. Let's also soak up the nourishment, and let it connect to your heart and soul. With that, our spirit will walk with the Holy Ghost.

Victory is ours! We have power, and in
this fight, we don't stand alone!

<u>God Bless</u>

Chapter 18

Where Did Evil Really Come From

I listened closely in Church, and did some reading about where evil came from. Although I read God created evil, I say Christ could have not made something so impure. I asked out loud, "How did Satan make his way, and be here?" I could not decide what to believe, and the more I thought about it, this is what **I think** could have happened.

Can it be possible, that at the time Lucifer was watching God create with, so much love and power, He also gave His angels wisdom and knowledge? As Lucifer watched, and taking everything in, he started desiring and wanting this power, not in a peaceful way. He really didn't need it, but only for greed. Lucifer saw the beautiful garden as a place to rule like a god. He also used the knowledge of the Holy Mountain, and wisdom from heaven.

In his day, which God created, he wanted it all. This selfish wanting is why evil manifested itself. Again, evil started out of greed. It's possible, right? Envy! Jealousy! Covenant! This was his need to have complete power over all, even the Creator. Once this started, Lucifer was imagining Christ kneeling before him. Though Christ was above all, He never flexed His power. He only showed shining love, never walking over the hearts of His angels. Christ hugged only their hearts, with loving hands and words.

Once this all started, Lucifer's hatred built itself up. Why? Who knew these feelings were the makings of evil? I read of the dragon, serpent and the demons. I believe demons are followers, who, came from heaven as falling angels, cast down as Lucifer. The dragons and serpents, can they be what Lucifer created? This could have been a way of bringing them forward, to try to overtake heaven and Christ for himself. This also could have been his dark mind, and black heart at work.

After all, he is not as powerful as Christ, but as one of the high ranking angel in heaven. We must never underestimate him. As the Bible warns, because he is master of disguises, and master over all illusions, chief of lies, and he also gains power from those who chooses to follow him. Every time someone turns to God, Lucifer is weakened. His rank in heaven use to be the bearer of light, now he is known for only darkness.

Once a beautiful angel, if you look real close, he is dark, and has ugly scars from being evil, master of sorrow. All of his power is dark, no light. When Lucifer smiles, it's with evil, and when he gets you to follow him, he's laughing at God. He can never provoke Christ, but he continues to try. Isn't this all evil? Can it be where evil raised its head?

*Do not be overcome by evil, but overcome evil with good. Romans 12:21 NKJV

It makes one wonder, was Lucifer ever happy? How can you walk, and look upon someone so wonderful, and loving as Christ? Yet, he still demands more. I see heaven as a place of peace and love, never pain or sorrow. So why would you need more? Mankind was not a big helper. Maybe it was ignorance in the beginning with Adam and Eve, but now, we know today, man has wisdom for God's will.

Lucifer continues to aid evil, dividing the world by claiming ourselves kings. They make others their servants, and being president, and ruling without a heart. Brothers divided us, claiming to be enemies, leading, God's children into war. We also see those making up their own religion, besides casting out those who we deem unworthy, and not lending a hand to thy neighbor. Do you realize, this is like back to being the Romans? Remember, they enslaved God's children, and damaged them with hate. They also taught from the dark world. Yes, Lucifer is the beginning of evil. Yes, we are helping him. This is why the priority is to steal, not give, pain and sorrow, not happiness and laugher. Why do we teach punishment, not forgiveness, and nearly always to turn their backs on mistakes, not compassion.

We teach to hate without cause, giving no mercy, just because of being different. Is it about whether it is religion, or color, along with ignorance? Why do we not care about anything? We need to teach what the heart means. We also see and demand the hopes and dreams evil men call this freedom. I call this, bondage! Is this not evil? Lucifer is behind it all, using man as a vessel against God.

Looking at all this, we get sicker and sicker, until the fever takes lives. As an example, our children are mostly controlled, not all, but more than it should be. They have yet to learn of God's teachings, only the dark side. They haven't learned of God's love, and know nothing of praise and goodness. That cycle continues from generation to generation, and gaining followers. Lucifer put up an illusion, so you can't see that there is a beautiful, wonderful world, with love. He only allows you to see the dark. But, you can break through the bondage, and use the key to the chains, if you want to see beauty. Lucifer doesn't want you to feel Christ's love! Take a big, deep breath, and say from the heart, **"I believe"** and just turn to the right.

Where you're standing, just turn, and look up, and have faith. You won't wait long. You will be filled up, and you will feel at peace. This is what Lucifer works so hard to keep from you. If we work together as one, and cast him from earth, as he was from heaven, there would be no places to go. If you turn to Lucifer, he infects everything he touches. If he doesn't plant his seeds, there is no reward for him. Remember, his happiness is you suffering. His battle is about power, not love.

So, as the verses say ...

***Be sober, be vigilant; because your adversary the devil walks about like a roaring lion,
seeking whom he may devour.
*Resist him, steadfast in the faith, knowing that the same sufferings are experienced by
your brotherhood in the world. 1 Peter 5:8-9 NKJV**

Lucifer may walk the earth bringing darkness and remember, he has demons that watch and listen. Darkness is in his sight, but we have a weapon, if we choose Christ, and if, we walk with Christ. If Christ is in our hearts, He becomes the candle that lights the way. It's a light that never goes out. Even Lucifer has no power to blow out the light. Faith starts from the heart, and when we speak, it must be from the heart. So, remember, do not roar, but sing instead, as a child of God.

Believe the words you speak, this is the key to success. Remember, Lucifer is master of everything dark. He can also disguise himself as a loved one. So, his goal is hate, you must go over his head with prayer. Don't let darkness guide you through life. Carry the candle of Christ daily.

Lucifer has been around far too long. We must go back, and return on the right side of the road. Light all candles in honor of Christ. Give praise, thanking the Father, and the Son, for thinking we are worthy to be saved.

Did you know your tongue can be life or death, because it starts from the heart? Do you truly believe in God, and Jesus? Be sure what your hearts says. If you speak out loud, remember, Lucifer can't read your mind but he listens. Don't forget the angry lion. Heaven is secure, thanks to the Archangels. Now, we must secure earth. I see some of the garden.

We can rebuild the rest. It won't be the same, but better. With faith and love secured in our hearts, it's never too late. Nothing is beyond God's mercy, you only need to step up, and take His hand. You can't see it, until you open your heart. Remember, heaven never closes. God sent Jesus, no one is left behind, unless you choose to stay. **<u>JOIN NOW,</u>** Not on the day of judgement!

If your heart believes, you can see the path Jesus took to the Father. Lucifer tries to take so much from us. He did so, on an empty promise. I'm not blaming him for all, because had mankind just trusted, the garden would still be ours. We would be at peace with Christ, walking in His love, not fighting to keep it.

Since that's gone, we must have faith, and believe Christ within. We are safe in His arms, and once we have faith and believe, we will see victory. Once again, walk in the garden that was lost to man. Lucifer's untruths and illusions are still trying to keep us out of reach. We must do as the Bible says. Always remember, it is full of God's wisdom. Don't let evil overcome you.

We can defeat it by doing this …
When someone shows you their ugly
side, show them God's beauty.
When someone throws a stone, catch it,
and use it to build a place of peace.
When someone is acting evil, give them
a reward with an act of love.
If they need food, share yours.
If they need water, offer your cup.
When someone is cussing you out, give words of wisdom.
When your enemy raises a weapon, stand
tall, wearing the armor of Christ.
Raise the flag of peace.
When someone refuses to believe, give
prayer for their heart and soul.
If your enemy seem hot from the sun,
offer the shade of Christ.

We are building our faith, not just for courage, but strength to stand. We are casting doubt from our world, to build our will, to continue to come with faith and the belief, we will see our Father.

I believe this journey is not going to be easy. It will not happen overnight, but because we step forward, and call His name, we are on the road to recovery. We can control our destiny, and have choices. I compare it to the pure blue sea, because I have blessings. I face it without fear.

"My Lord Christ is above me, and I cross the sea with faith. I believe my Lord is my bridge to safety. When evil blows a breath, heavy winds come. When evil brings heavy rains and storms, it turns into serious conflict. The rain comes down like a sharp knife, and when evil stomps its feet, the world shakes violently. <u>I show no fear!</u> <u>Love has no fear!</u> I keep my faith and beliefs! I only see Jesus turning these things to good. The wind becomes a vacuum to clear the air, while the stormy rain is use to wash and purify."

High up in the air, the shaking of the earth helps harvest the fruit. The ice from the storms is used to cool the air, when it becomes to hot, making it comfortable. We are able to take all that Lucifer throws in our path, and turn it around for the good of man.

* "Let not your heart be troubled; you believe in God, believe also in Me.
John 14:1 NKJV

When evil comes, look at it as a positive thing. Why? Just turn it around. Remember, don't fight evil with evil, you don't win that way. Again, fight evil with love, and faith in Christ. There are so many positive things we can do, and say, to bring love to our neighbors. Conquer evil! Lucifer sees it, but he continues to fight, even though he's losing the battle.

I completely believe everything I have said. It's not the full story, or the way you may tell it. One thing that is always the same, is faith and belief in **Jehovah-Nissi, and the Messiah.**

So, I hope that whatever story you choose to follow, you, as I, will keep trying to climb the Holy Mountain, and reach the top. We shall walk in the glory of His love, and be at peace.

*Now may the God of hope fill you with all joy and peace in believing, that you may
abound in hope by the power of the Holy Spirit. Romans 15:13 NKJV

<u>Be Bless On Your Journey!</u>

Chapter 19

Why Lucifer's Take Over Failed

I believe after Lucifer's fall to earth, his plan was not just to conquer, destroy God's beautiful garden, but spread his demons around the world. His aim was to plant his seeds of sin. He tried to use God's definition of sin, to attack man and woman separately. The first time he used curiosity in Eve, and the love Adam had for Eve.

Using a disguise, Lucifer made himself look different. Secondly, he inserted himself in man's life, by making man see ugly things and imperfections everywhere, especially the home. These are the illusions of sin, Lucifer made up to confuse man. He also made woman lose respect for herself. He made them believe they needed to add to themselves to be beautiful, and seeking artificial ways, not seeing the beauty.

God made them from love. Man had to think they had to go against a promise given to a partner. So, it made them feel important, to boost their pride, and know their heart. This is Lucifer's plan for woman, too. Lucifer made them think this is dishonest and disloyal, or a woman breaking a promise, because she thinks she needs reassurance.

He also made woman let their flesh rule their mind and body, putting the heart and soul with spirit in a dark place, without any light. What man and woman forgot, is Lucifer has no mercy, just disguises. He also looks to distract you. He can't read your mind, so he listens, and uses his demons too. Remember, it's a sin to think of wrong things, even when you don't speak it. The tongue can be life or death, so speak from Christ.

*Death and life are in the power of the tongue, and those who love it will eat its fruit.
Proverbs 18:21 NKJV

Lucifer works hard against you, making it hard to see the beauty God has created. He makes loud noises, so you are unable to hear the music from Heaven. So, listen close with Christs' ears! Lucifer does not wish for you to know that God created man and woman different for a reason. God has created a garden of beauty, with different flowers and trees of all shapes and sizes. The garden also included beautiful color lights, to give it a variety of completeness.

God created from His heart, with love being a place of peace and tranquility. Christ wanted to watch His garden, and prosper, and letting the heart and soul with the spirit stay the same in all. God does not create imperfections, only perfections. In man, God strived for excellence. Lucifer does the opposite for woman. He makes her feel too thin or to fat, unworthy, and a shame to be seen. He also makes woman see she's too dark, or too white, or red with freckles.

Woman sees ugly, and they begin to covet others. Why? It keeps them from seeing the beauty of the Creator, because it keeps them off balance. You need to get balance with Christ, to gain your senses, and to be sturdy. Look hard at God's creation, and see beauty. Lucifer made man think he needs to paint symbols on themselves, to show their strength and man hood.

* 'You shall not make any cuttings in your flesh for the dead, nor tattoo any marks on
you: I am the LORD. Leviticus 19:28 NKJV

Lucifer also saw an opening in the new generation of our young. He saw them as leaders of the righteous, so he planted a negative seed in the man and woman of today. He hoped it would guide the young his way. Lucifer is leaving no stone unturned. Man is failing to see this conspiracy, working on his looks and possessions, instead of **heart, soul and spirit.**

Lucifer's goal is leading them to darkness. This plan is still working. We must stop, and get back to basics, and find the path of Christ again. First off, start looking for Jesus' hand, asking forgiveness and mercy. Secondly, woman needs to stop looking in man's mirror. Look through Christ, and see God's work, for He is the **Author and Creator.** He only creates beauty.

Man needs to remember who he is, under Christ. Remember, strength comes from the heart, and being strong, is in the soul of glory. Being manly isn't as important, but the spirit in Christ and pride is what you have, in loving the Father and the Son.

Woman should know the flesh does not have control. It's a choice, and beauty is in the eyes of Christ. Remember, the word "ugly" came from evil. However, it can be erase with love. I know you are beautiful, so see yourself through the eyes of Jesus!

We must stop, and stand face to face with our demons. Fight, with the weapon God sent through Jesus, the weapon of love and peace, covered by Christ. I say to Lucifer, "You were created by God." He created Heaven and Earth, the **Author and Master.**

<u>**Today, we will take the shades off the windows, and expose you in Jesus name …**</u>
* You will not hold God's people in bondage!
* There is no one higher than Christ!
* You may not walk on the Holy Mountain!
* Your privileges have been revoked!
* We will have protection under the Holy Ghost for our young!

Beauty is once again in the eyes of Christ, our Lord. He has sent a reflection of himself, and this is what I see in the mirror. Lucifer, I no longer hear your noise, that you call music. I can hear the Holy Ghost singing the gospel.

I Say …
"Thank You God, for sending man Jesus. Thank You Jesus for saving man's life again. You are truly merciful."

Lucifer chose to forget the wonders of God, and His love for all. He also gave him life and put him high up in rank. Lucifer exists on greed, and who he is today. Today, Lucifer wants man to give up God's blessings, and be as he - - empty as a shell. He wishes man, not to see the beauty of the earth and the miracles of life. Lucifer wishes man to turn off the lights, and stand in the darkness, confuse of where to walk, because we cannot see. Lucifer made a choice to be who he is, and wants to take control.

We are taking it back! We have a path! That will, give life and turn right! Don't you dare believe, you don't have a choice! We all know God is the Creator, and Author. He gives a choice to you, and all you need is to believe, and have faith with trust.

I chose the light over darkness. I chose colors of wonder and music from the Gospel. You must believe! If I have a choice, so do you!

<u>Be Blessed!</u>

Chapter 20

Pray With Me

*Cast your burden on the LORD, and He shall sustain you; He shall never permit the righteous to be moved. Psalm 55:22 NKJV

Jesus is so mighty! He carries the burdens of all, and it does not weigh Him down. He still agonizes over your burdens. He will never turn away, because He is that merciful and forgiven.

*For unto us a Child is born, unto us a Son is given; and the government will be upon His shoulder. And His name will be called Wonderful, Counselor, Mighty God, Everlasting Father, Prince of Peace. Isaiah 9:6 NKJV

Reach for Jesus, don't be an empty shell of a man. Be somebody, be the child of God. What do you have to lose? If you're not winning your way, try Jesus. Live in glory. Let me give you some prayers:

<u>Pray With Me-First Prayer:</u>
"I want to thank You Jesus for a new day, and I know, each and every day, You're blessings are always greater than the last. I also want to thank You for given me mercy, even though I have slipped off the path. You love me anyway, Jesus. Thank You for being who You are, the <u>Anointed One</u>. "You showed mercy and love to someone broken, because it has set me free, I'm able to testify, so that those who are

nonbelievers, may know You. Thank You Jesus, just thank You, for You are my rock. You are also someone I can depend on, and will stand with me, even at my worse. You've wiped my tears, and drowned my sins away, and gave me life.

"I have a new soul and spirit, thank You, even though I have many burdens. You took me in your arms, despite my illnesses, tears and my worries. You calmed my sorrows, making them Yours. I have surrendered all, not keeping anything for myself. Jesus, You deserve praise and glory, for Your work is so much more, than any man can imagine.

"So, anything I can do, I say thank You, for You are the Master and the Creator, the Author of this story, in the name of the Father and the Son-Amen."

*Keep your heart with all diligence, for out of it spring the issues of life.
Proverbs 4:23 NKJV

<u>Pray With Me-Second Prayer:</u>
"I would also like to say, thank You, for the courage You given me. So, I may stand up with my shoulders back and my head held high, facing evil, and staring him in the eyes so, he cannot see me, but see your face Lord, and evil will know. I don't stand alone. Thank You for covering me with love, and showing evil there's nothing left for him.

Thank You for Your trust in me, and I trust You, Lord. So, when evil knocks on the door, I let You answer. Evil knows he is not welcome here in this home. I thank You Jesus, for when I was sick, You were the blanket that the nurse put on me. There was nowhere for evil to lie down. I thank You Jesus, because the man across the way said, "There's no more room, and there is no helping hands."

It seemed hopeless, and You reached out, and kept me warm. Your words of hope built, and showed me hope. I'm not weary, and You shined Your light. All of that gave me a shelter, and I was welcomed. I knew it was Your gift, to someone beaten down by man. I was someone who slipped off Your path, but You showed me mercy.

Today I see the love You have for mankind, so thank You Jesus, I say out loud, <u>"Hallelujah!"</u> I will sing out my praises, Your words will be my guidance to the Kingdom. I will pray day and night, thank You Jesus, Amen."

* "Let not your heart be troubled; you believe in God, believe also in Me.
John 14:1 NKJV

<u>Pray With Me-Third Prayer:</u>
"Jesus, You are not just an awesome God, but the Almighty One. I will do my best Lord to walk the path, for I have seen the <u>Golden Mile</u>. I have faith in You. I have myself, which is from Your teaching. I ask for guidance from You, to show me how I may live in Your word. Jesus, my heart is Yours to command, and my faith is strong in Love for You.

My spirit awaits Your will, and my mind bleeds into my heart. Jesus, You are the Anoint One, and should be given praises, and we should be celebrating Your name. Jesus, there are so many ways You are honored by prayer, or by song, even through dance. Most of all, we trust and believe in Your love, and have faith.

I hope one day man will prove his worth, but for now Jesus, we're not only asking You for guidance, but forgiveness and mercy. We ask not only for ourselves, but for all mankind. So, they too can feel whole and complete, not empty as a shell. You are the Messiah, my Lord, and the only One who can deliver us from evil. Lord Jesus, You are the key to the Kingdom, because it is You we pass through to the Father, who awaits mankind-Amen."

*Surely goodness and mercy shall follow me all the days of my life; and I will dwell in the
house of the LORD forever. Psalm 23:6 NKJV

Chapter 21

Bible Study

I went to Bible study for the first time in years. I learned so much, and after the Pastor had us stand, he said a prayer over everyone. As I walked home, I was thinking of what I learned. Then, I realized how dark it was outside. I asked God to please help me get home safely. When I got to the stores, which were all closed, someone, I did not know, came up behind me. They said, "Keep walking!"

I was so scared, I could not speak at first. Then, I started thinking, should I run, but what if they have a gun? I also started looking for someone, seeking help. When "We" got to my street, I started praying out loud. I came to a field, I dropped to my knees, and prayed louder. A friend and his mother appeared, and asked me if everything was ok?

When I raised my head and looked around, I was alone, only the street light was shining. When I looked closer, it was shining on a Bible, which I had dropped when praying. I believe God walked me home. What do you think?

*For we walk by faith, not by sight. 2 Corinthians 5:7 NKJV

* "Ask, and it will be given to you; seek, and you will find; knock, and it will be opened to you. Matthew 7:7 NKJV

I only needed faith and to believe in Christ.

<u>A Direction To The Path:</u>

Always keep faith on your right side, and trust in your beliefs. Trust in your heart and Christ in your soul. Courage is your shield, and your mind on Jesus. Your voice must speak only praises. Your feet go on the path of the righteous. When you have all of this, you will find peace. Be strong in this, and do not lose faith, for these things are the way to the Father, and the victory to the promise land.

*** "This Book of the Law shall not depart from your mouth, but you shall meditate in it
day and night, that you may observe to do according to all that is written in it. For
then you will make your way prosperous, and then you will have good success.
Joshua 1:8 NKJV**

*For *"He who would love life and see good days, let him refrain his tongue from evil, and his
lips from speaking deceit.
*Let him turn away from evil and do good; let him seek peace and pursue it.
*For the eyes of the Lord are on the righteous, and His ears are open to their prayers; But
the face of the Lord is against those who do evil."* **1 Peter 3:10-12 NKJV**

Chapter 22

Strong Tools

Here's something to think about, for those unbelievers, or those who lost their faith. It easily could be you. When you lose a love one you may feel betrayed, it could be you. Just don't believe in what you can't see, and you're unsure of what you feel. When your faith is shaky, God understands. You should know, the Father and the Son would never betray you. I want to give you food for thought. God stands with us, even when we have loss faith. His mercy and forgiveness is at arm's reach.

I was thinking of my own life, and those of my children, and their lives. We must think of what kind of signal we send to them. They inherit our tools, and if our tools are damage or miss guided, the homes we build are not solid. They cannot withstand the storm that comes. If, our children use the same tools, they too can't build a solid home. We must use the tools God sent to mankind.

There are times our children get lost, and we see the pain they are suffering. I've been there, evil has climbed the fence, and inserted himself. His roots are growing, don't let this stop you on your path. **Pray!** God is working on it. Nothing is impossible. It can all be turned around. Use your tools through Jesus, because through Jesus Christ, the tools give the courage and strength. With this, we stand strong on Holy Ground.

Remember, the tools and materials we pass to our children can stand strong, even in a storm. So, it's not always what you see, or the loss of a love one, God would not betray your faith in Him. His love and Blessings proves that He stands with us.

We must believe, and we must see through the eyes of Christ. All our love ones also went to homes they built, using strong tools. They in turn, pass the tools that are strong, in order to build homes.

The children should also know, this takes commitment and hard work along the path. For every step we take, evil tries to stop us. Despite challenges, if we trust in Jesus, we can build with the right tools. If we believe, and have faith in Christ, we must also trust what our heart tells us. If we continue to not believe, then the faith will fade, and what we built no matter the price, we pay it.

Be strong, because the tools we use are not always useful and have been damaged. They lead to the home becoming doomed. It's easy to be invaded by, "Pirates of Sin." These Pirates have no mercy or remorse, nor heart or soul. The storm that comes with these Pirates is dark, but this is not final. We can redeem ourselves through Jesus Christ.

We just need to reach for our faith and believe. So, you see, it's not what you see, but what you believe. Know there is hope, and you can dream. Just keep strong tools, It is your given right through Christ, that you can have a happy home.

Be Blessed On Your Journey To Jesus

Chapter 23

The Way To Freedom

Jesus saves lives, never seeing the outer shell, only the inner beauty. With love, Jesus is the guide to Christ. You can't reach this goal without Jesus, for He is the key to the door of the Kingdom. Through Jesus, we are face to face with the Father. We treasure the memories of the miracles done yesterday, and the ones given today.

We have a chance to repent for our sins, and receive forgiveness from the Father. Secondly, we find that the dead are not dead, but have been set free of the world. When the shells of sin are gone from the path, the spirit and soul are free of man's bondage. With forgiveness, we can move forward. We place all of our hopes and dreams, in our sprit and soul. We also offer ourselves to Jesus, because without this offering, there will be no hopes or dreams.

We give thanks to Christ for loving man, enough that He finds man worthy, and not falling away from earth. Even when we start over with a fresh new world, He still gives man a chance to clean up the sin. Yes, He loves with care so if you have any hopes and dreams, have them of Christ. Sometimes, we labor all day, and don't feel we are getting anywhere. **Stop!** Don't go left, its evil creating illusions to block your path to the right to God.

God sees and hears all your labor. Look close! **A job well done children!** Listen and look to Christ's love, and see every day, we wake up refresh, it's a blessing, until we are home in the Kingdom of God's love.

OH, clap your hands, all you peoples! Shout to God with the voice of triumph!
Psalm 47:1 NKJV

We Are Not Lost, There Is Hope:

We have many lost days which bring sadness, but if we reach for the hand of Jesus, we can find happiness. With joy in the world, there are still days of sorrow, but we replace it, and bring in hope with mercy. We remember the day of being reborn, and submerged in the blessed water, that served as the blood of Jesus. We also get forgiveness from the Father. You should never feel lost again, even though evil puts temptation in our path. Evil fades without taking root, because we have found our way back to the path, through Jesus.

Our vow to Jesus is to work hard, and live in the word of Christ. If we are wise, we will never make the same mistake again, but we move forward to be better in life. In the will of God, and with this courage, we will move forward, and find joy from heaven and the word.

Sorrow, weakness, weightlessness, bondage, hate, and pain will be gone forever. They won't have a place in this world, because to live through Jesus, is a blessing and everlasting life. We need to stay focus on God, so we don't slip off the path. It is a battle, but it's worth the work. So, **stand with the flag of peace, and stand in victory.**

I'm Here:

I stand before you saying, look at me, **I'M HERE!** I'm not just here, but living. I've seen trouble and disappointment and hate. Besides, I've known sadness. I have heard hateful laughter and

I've been in pain, but nothing can make me fall. I stand today, tall and strong. I laugh and I'm happy, I'm here.

I saw the water rise and felt the earth shake. Nothing can make me fall, I'm still standing. I hold my head up high, proud of myself, and not ashamed of being a child of God. I own my faith. It can't be turned around, not by man or beast. I'm here, believing and with knowledge. I must embrace the world, and not let others decide how I'm going to live. I'm here with love and compassion in my heart. I have a positive attitude, and a strong will! I will approach everything that way, because I have God on my side, and I'm here to stay!

*It is good to give thanks to the LORD, and to sing praises to Your name, O Most High;
*To declare Your lovingkindness in the morning, and Your faithfulness every night.
Psalm 92:1-2 NKJV

*DELIVER me from my enemies, O my God; defend me from those who rise up against me. Psalm 59:1 NKJV

I'm still standing, Lord I will sing of Your strength in the morning. I will sing of Your love, for You are my fortress, refuge and strength in times of trouble. Thank You, my Lord Christ. I'm standing, I survived the storm. I faced the enemy and won!

Glory Hallelujah! Thank You Jesus!

Chapter 24

Finding My Way Back

I have been very distant to the Church, with no excuse, and believing I'm not worthy to be in the presents of the Lord. Because of this doubt, evil was able to step in and plant seeds. The seeds created weariness, and weighed me down. My heart and soul got disconnected from my mind, so only half of my body was functioning. That half was becoming empty, too.

When this happens, you can't sort things out, and I know something needed to be done, before there was no way back from darkness. The darkness was making me **"blind."** My strength was leaving me, and emptiness was becoming my partner. Trying to find my way, I was feeling lost, and confused. I asked myself, why I was falling asleep with my dreams.

Then, I felt a spark in me. I'm not sure how, but I began to float in my dreams. I felt a connection, although very small, but it was there. I also felt peace and hope. When I awoke the next day, I was a little lighter. It was enough to be reconnected to my heart and soul.

When I went to church that morning, I knew the sermon was directed at me. It made me feel welcome, back in the house of Christ. I called out to Jesus, and found my faith. I was still a bit unsure, and to my surprise, Jesus showed me, I will always be welcomed in the house of Christ. I found great peace come over me. Jesus, you see, has surrounded me, and I remembered the words spoken to all men.

Jesus said ...

*** "And if I go and prepare a place for you, I will come again
and receive you to Myself;
that where I am, there you may be also.
* "And where I go you know, and the way you know." John
14:3-4 NKJV**

I now realize Jesus never left man alone, I just needed to keep
faith, and trust in Him, and myself. Besides, I knew I had to
live in the word even in His absence. I forgot to stand strong.
Thinking I was alone without His presences, I forget to keep
faith without sight. You just have to believe. Our hearts need
faith, while He is preparing a place. I was to stay strong in faith.
I knew, if I needed Him, I just needed to call out, and fear
nothing. Christ is my protector! You see, Jesus knows that evil
will try to always insert himself. So, you are blocked from Jesus,
but prayer and faith, in our Christ, will be our safety. Beware,
for evil does surveillance, hoping for a chance to plant his seeds
of doubt, and spread sadness with pain in you. Bondage, with
chains, holds the spirit and soul captive in darkness. We must
never give up to evil.

He searches for a key weakness, so he may control us. **Don't
give into fear! Mankind has Christ! We will have the
victory!** I believe in God, and I have faith in the Son, and I
believe in the miracles of love. I confess, I have strayed from
the path. I make no excuses, and I got lost, because I was doing
it alone. Thank God, I found my way back, and He opened His
arms and showed me mercy through His Son, the Messiah.
I once again have hope of being free, and dreams of victory.
I feel so free, looking across the sea. I can once again take
many steps, and with no fear of falling, I can walk across to

the Kingdom, the Promise Land. I'm waiting for my judgment day, for I have repented, and open to Christ. I believe in myself once again. I have the answers to all who asked, **who am I?** I say to the world, **I am a child of God.** I will walk the green miles set before me.

I am keeping my faith for Jesus, as well as His love as my shield. I know Jesus stands with me in the storm. I pledge to work sun up to sun down, glorifying His name, and holding to the commandments close to my heart. I will seek comfort, only from the Holy Ghost, in the name of the Father, and as spoken by Jesus.

* **"But that the world may know that I love the Father, and as the Father gave Me**
commandment, so I do. Arise, let us go from here. John 14:31 NKJV

So yes, I follow Jesus to the Holy place. One day, after my journey, I can receive everlasting life. On my journey, I will not stray from my commandments. I will keep my heart turned to the heavens, and never look down. Initially, I washed in the blood of Jesus. As I continue, I will pray in the name of the Holy Ghost. This is my goal, keeping the peace Jesus has blessed me with, and to all mankind.

* **"Do you not believe that I am in the Father, and the Father in Me? The words that I**
speak to you I do not speak on My own authority; but the Father who dwells in Me
does the works. John 14:10 NKJV

I finely understand all the words spoken to me. We must continue to study the Bible, and learn of His love. Always be up lifted, so you know all, and see good and bad. Remember, every day is a new day, as all yesterdays are gone. **Blessings start new every day.**

Feel the love, don't question the gifts. When Jesus speaks of the journey, or God's commandments He sent down to man, embrace the glory! I myself need to study, and learn to keep peace within me. Why? It keeps the storms away! Studying the Bible daily is reassuring for all mankind.

Our work we do for Christ is very rewarding. When I think of the end of the journey, I'm very excited. At long last, I can be free of the world's bondage on me. I have no hardships to bare. Sin will be no more, only a memory. For the first time, I can see my way to the Kingdom. Following Christ, I will start training, and helping others, in the army that is rising up.

Through the Holy Christ, we will not just break chains, we will tear down walls. Victory will be ours. I just don't feel it, I see it. Standing with Jesus, I may not be as tall, but I'm taller than the world. With the love of Jesus, I stand wiser today then yesterday. I will not stop reading the book of knowledge God has sent to us. Every time I open it, I see and feel stronger. There is no ending of the word, or its knowledge. Every day, is new. Come receive your share of the blessings, and you can glorify in His spirit and love.

Be Blessed!

Chapter 25

A Journey

On my journey, I have learned to believe in myself. My trust in Jesus is as solid as a rock. Jesus believes in me, with a true heart and soul. I will never doubt Jesus' guidance on my journey. My strength comes from Jesus. His torch is so bright, and it will beckon me to fellow. It is truly the light from heaven.

I will have strength and compassion to comfort me, when weariness tries to step in my path. Jesus continues to give me guidance, even when weakness of the flesh and ignorance, tries to darken my path. I prefer to see how the journey is teaching me to live. The mercy of Jesus will be there to stand with me.

Jesus' faith has filled me, and all I want to do, is surrender to Him.

My journey is also teaching me to use my heart for love. I am not bitter, and my soul will not be envious. The "Neighbors" and I will not give the gift of life away. My journey, with prayer, shows who I should be, and what not to be, for I am the child of God.

*Let us therefore come boldly to the throne of grace, that we may obtain mercy and find
grace to help in time of need. Hebrews 4:16 NKJV

My journey, with faith in Christ, gave me encouragement, and the confidence in myself. I can face evil, and on my journey, mankind has shown me that there are times, they focus on the mistakes, rather than lending a helping hand. Well, my journey with Jesus has never showed disappointment, I go forward with that.

When I turn left, not right, Jesus always showed love for me. When I stay inside the shell, not the outer, that taught me what Christ, our Lord, is all about. I wish to say, "Thank You Jesus, from the bottom of my heart, because You have showed me so many times what the mercy is all about."

My journey also shows what Jesus has done for all mankind. Jesus suffered and sacrificed for mankind, never holding a grudge or hatred. Even after we sin, He has stood by mankind with love and doing it since the beginning of time. On my journey, I wish to praise Him, but work harder to be who He wishes mankind to be. It has also been a learning one, and I hope, I am who I should be.

* "And you shall know the truth, and the truth shall make you free." John 8:32 NKJV

Thank You Jesus, for the guidance. I can see the bridge from here, with the beckon of Christ's light shining. I realize I must complete my journey, while keeping the faith. This is my way to the Kingdom. You must find yours, by standing by faith.

<u>May You Be Blessed</u>

Chapter 26

Resist

*Therefore submit to God. Resist the devil and he will flee from you.
James 4:7 NKJV

Before my God, I will fight to resist evil, and bow down to no one. God is my only resource for forgiveness. I will raise my head, and look to the heavens for mercy. I asked my God, not to do the work for me, but to show me the right door. I am ready to take the challenge, and enter, and be ready to work, doing His will.

I will try to keep only praise for my Lord. This is an honor, because there is no glory to be had. Before our God, I resist evil, and it must come from the heart. I also resist what is laid before me, which is not from the Kingdom. Speaking for myself, I'm not perfect, or strong, but I try to be. There are times I make mistake. Things sometimes are made to look good, but I find evil in the path. Evil comes in different ways, but God knows this illusion evil uses on man. God is always there to forgive.

God has sent a book, with a mirror we look in, to help us, so we can see evil for what he is. That is why it's always a battle. Just so you know, we are winning, so don't give up. Together, we will win, and together we are strong. I believe evil will flee from man, if we stay united as one. Keep God in your heart and soul. Let's win this battle together, blessings to you. If there is resistance, just put on the armor of God. Blessings flow, even though evil tries to take them away. He will be met with the hand of God, with this, we can stand strong and hold our ground.

As it's written in Peter ...

*Be sober, be vigilant; because your adversary the devil walks about like a roaring lion,
seeking whom he may devour.
*Resist him, steadfast in the faith, knowing that the same sufferings are experienced by
your brotherhood in the world.
1 Peter 5:8-9 NKJV

Mind, Heart, Soul, Spirt, in and of itself will not protect you, and only the armor of God, working as one, will protect you. Don't forget to pray, and stay diligent. He comes in all disguises and forms, looking helpful at times. No matter what, Christ will always prevail.

So, when I say, be on guard, it means stay on your journey, and always study the word of God. It is up lifting, and remember, the path to Jesus is always to the right. There are no left turns! The Bible always puts the path to the right. You should also live a pure life.

It takes work, but evil then, will not be able to cross lines, because the blood of Jesus, your love, and trust in Him, will shield you always.

*You are hiding place and my shield; I hope in Your word.
Psalm 119:114 NKJV

IT CAN BE DONE!

Chapter 27

I Wish Dreams Came True

I'm looking at myself, trying to look past my former shell. The **"Window Cleaner"** that I use is called **"Happiness"**. When the sun shines within, it will push the darkness out. I also open the doors, so the breath of God may **"Vacuum"** out the weariness in the air. Suffering should also go **"Packing"**, never to be felt again. God's mercy is also the best **"Medicine"** the body can take. It relieves the pain, and heals all wounds.

I also draw the blood of Jesus, using it as a **"Curtain"** for protection from evil. While sleeping I wish to clean house, leaving nothing that would block my path to God. Today, I am also stopping the infection from sin using **"Faith"**. My faith also prevents no more bleeding from the mind, which if it had advanced, would have made it to the heart. It would have also affected my soul and spirit. I have the will, and my faith is my strength, and my spirit is strong, as well as nourished. I will have victory, because I refuse to hold on to yesterdays! God has given me many blessings, and I won't waste them on emptiness.

***The things which you learned and received and heard and saw in me, these do, and the
God of peace will be with you. Philippians 4:9 NKJV**

This gives me strength to say to Satan, "Step aside, I'm coming through!" I am walking in victory with God's hands and guidance. This will always come true, when I put God first, not just once but always. I wish to praise God, with singing and dancing out loud, so the heavens can hear me.

My faith and steps will also in able me to walk across the sea, using the bridge, made from the cross. It was use to free man, so it will lead me to the Kingdom. I have made a lot of wishes, and with prayer each is grantee. My wishes are what is written in love, and comes from my heart and soul. A wish is not always about riches, but in Christ, that proves you are dreaming of a joyful life.

You must have faith, so when you do wish, in your dreams, put Christ first. Watch and listen! Even having sinful thoughts, will relinquish themselves, and your wishes will come true. It's not a dream after all, it's free blessings to you. There's a song that inspires me.

I recall the words of <u>Tasha Cobbs</u> song <u>"You Know My Name,"</u> which refers to <u>important words of faith ...</u>

No fire can burn me
No battle can turn me
No mountain can stop me
'Cause You hold my hand
And I'm walking in Your victory
'Cause Your power is within me
No giant can defeat me
'Cause You hold my hand

<u>My Blessing:</u>

I have a God who knows the truth about me, and took me under His wing. My God knows everything I have done, and still loves me. My God will always stand by me, and holds me tightly, in His hands. My God showed me I'm also worthy, even though I'm not perfect. My God knows I'll never lie to Him, because if I do, it would be to myself, for He knows all. I always find myself trying to be faithful, and trust with all my being. This is the gift I give to God, who gave His Son for me. I have a God who believes in me, enough that He will always be with me. God trusts me, even though, sometimes I don't deserve it. He also trusts me without doubt. His love is unconditional, day after day. I give all my heart and soul to my God, that's my gift to Him. My gift will be mercy, forgiveness and life.

*The Lord is merciful and gracious, slow to anger, and abounding in mercy.
Psalm 103:8 NKJV

*He heals the brokenhearted and binds up their wounds.
Psalm 147:3 NKJV

Chapter 28

A Prayer For All

I am bowing my head, and given glory to God, the Son and Father. I ask that You reach down, and give blessings to all families and friends. So, You also show mercy to strangers, that are of the family of Christ. Bless those lost and the unbelievers, or those who have slipped off the path. I also ask You to lay hands on the children of the world, barring any evil or weapons raised against them. We only let them see only through the blood of Jesus.

Secondly, we ask forgiveness for all sins, and even those who are not worthy of Your love. Thirdly, we ask to be blessed and we thank You for the blessings. You have gifted us a life, which is the greatest gift of all. This will allow us to rise up, and stand strong, without doubt, or shame of who sees us wearing the armor of Christ. Raise the weapon, the flag of peace and love. It gives us hope in our hearts, and faith in our soul. It also gives strength to cast out Satan and his demons.

Lord, I know when I look to the heavens, I see smiles shining down on our faces. Father, help us to walk in Your glory, and the Holy Ghost, for when we walk, we are not claiming the glory, but seeing Your grace. We are seeing the fall of thy enemy, and Your smile for a job well done. In our sleep, may the sky open, and rain with the blood of Jesus, too, wash our soul, and connect us to You forever.

When we awake, all is right! Thank You for that Lord, for giving us a glorious gift of life. Both today and tomorrow, I surrender, all to You, Lord. Use me to do Your work, in the name of the Father and the Son-Amen.

*I thank my God upon every remembrance of you,
*always in every prayer of mine making request for you all
with joy,
*for your fellowship in the gospel from the first day until now,
*being confident of this very thing, that He who has begun
a good work in you will
complete it until the day of Jesus Christ;
*just as it is right for me to think this of you all, because I
have you in my heart, inasmuch
as both in my chains and in the defense and confirmation
of the gospel, you all are
partakers with me of grace. Philippians 1:3-7 NKJV

God Has Spoken, Just Listen:

God has spoken through Jesus, His Son. Every day is a new day through God, the Creator and Author. His will writes the story of the day. When I write my own story, I do it with faith and the love of my Lord Savior. So, as I write, my stories will bless me. I have a pure Heart, because He is with me in all things.
As I do, write your story of the day, and do it with the knowledge that your faith in Him will guide you forever. Don't look back, because God is before you. Make sure you have a blessed day, and know you are not alone.

I Stand With You:

On our journey, we also face rough times. I've had those too, but I've learned. Jesus will light the way, and we will rise above, because quitting is not an option, it's a choice. Failure is just a word, and can be erased. We will hold each other up, no one is alone. I'm here, and I stand with you.

<u>Giving Thanks:</u>

Have you thanked God today? Have you called to Jesus? Well, today I thank God for life, also for honoring me, by letting me walk this earth. With a chance to be redeemed, I will thank Him in death, because when it comes, the word death will erase itself. It will become eternal life. This is a very precious gift from God, promised through Jesus.

Chapter 29

Who Am I To You?

I will shield you from the fire, and you will not be burned. You will win all battles. There are no losers, only peace. **<u>You will walk in victory</u>!** You will also climb all Mountains. I will give you strength, and the power to defeat the dragon, or giant. There is no fear under the Holy Ghost. Listen to the trumpets, and rejoice by singing and dancing.

When you add to your hopes and dreams, they will become your stepping stones. I bring a message from Christ, for a job well done. He does not look for a perfect singer, or dancer, or one who knows how to put words together and pray. He really wants servants, who have a heart of love and compassion. Are you a servant with faith, and believes in Christ, and walks on the right side?

Are you also someone who knows what to do with the rocks that evil throws, or how to use the words spoken, that cause pain to the heart? What is needed in battle with evil? The weapons, and the power of glory, is within you. Christ loves you, take it with blessings of God.

Don't ever lose sight, because evil has illusions. Never be deceived, because you are greater than he. Serpent's heads will fall, because believers don't look down, or look over their shoulders. The journey for Christ stands before you. Blessings to you all, just believe, and keep hope and dreams in your heart.

Prayers With Hopes And Dreams:

I always thought my hopes and dreams would become true and everlasting. I have always put them in the hands of Christ. His power gives me strength.

I believe I can pray to Him and He will hear my prayers. I believe it's not my words that are important, but how they are spoken within my heart. I will keep my faith because it fills my soul. Rejoice!

I believe when you move forward with courage, Christ is by your side. I believe your spirit is always in flight. I'm at peace, like a clam wind blowing through the trees. I also believe you will always be under the love of the Father.

My journey has always had challenges. I have not faced them alone, because of my belief in Christ. Stand strong, and receive the blessings from Heaven, because there are no limits or payment due.

Blessings To You And Yours

Chapter 30

Christ Stands For You

A stranger drove into a small town, and went straight to Church on a Sunday morning. Arriving early, he parked. When he got out of the car, a smile crossed his face, as he saw the Church before him.

Half way to the entrance, he turned back, hearing a car's horn. He made eye contact with the car's driver. An old woman, lean out her window and said, "You can't park there it's for members only!" The stranger took his car out of the lot.

When in Church, the stranger sat in one of the middle seats. He appeared to be praying silently. Before the service started, a young man, with his wife and child, appeared at his side, and said, "Excuse me Sir you're in our seats!" The stranger smiled, and moved to the seats behind them. When the service started, the Pastor began with a prayer. He spoke loud and clear.

The Prayer:

"Father, I ask for mercy on those who are blind, and those who are stricken with arthritis. I pray, too, for those who are sick within, and those who are in despair about life's ups and down. I also pray, too, for those who are unbelievers, who are in need of Your love."

After the prayer, the stranger began to hold on to the seat in front of him, as if it was hard to stand. His eyes glaze over like a blind man, and his fingers became crooked with arthritis. You could also see, he was having trouble breathing, like someone with heart problems. As the Pastor continued praying, the congregation also became aware of the strangers deformities. The old woman from the parking lot said, "What's happening to you?" He looked at her, with love in his eyes. The young man and family turned, and by chance found themselves seated next to the stranger. By then, the entire congregation was looking on and listening. Falling to their knees, The Pastor said, **"Thank You Father!"**
That's when it happened! Everyone awoke in their beds, and it was Sunday Morning, all over again! Was it just a dream, or was it good and evil facing off?
A stranger drove into a small town, and went straight to Church on a Sunday morning. After parking, an old woman leans out

of her car and said, "Welcome!" The stranger said, "Blessings to you!"

In Church, the stranger sat in the middle seats. A young man, with his wife and child said, "Welcome we hope you enjoy the service!" The stranger felt the love and kindness of all the members in the Church. Everyone was in good spirits. However, one person was not happy. He believed if he gave them dark dreams, it would carry over. What he didn't realize, was the love of Christ watches over them while they sleep.

*Behold, He who keeps Israel shall neither slumber nor sleep. Psalm 121:4 NKJV

You have to know, evil can't win. When you have strong hearts, with Christ, all you need is trust and believe. So, your hopes and dreams will never have dark, or painful ways. We always have hopes of peace, dreams, and everlasting life. Evil must remember, our protector does not slumber.

The morale of this story is, I will stand under the right wing of Christ. I will stand strong with courage, and with the will of iron. My strength is solid. I will not bow down to lies and illusions. I stand on Christ's love.

Chapter 31

Remember Me In History

When your journey of life ends here on earth, what would you like told about you?

Would you be remembered for standing to the right, or left? Did you know, there are two paths in the road, the fork to the left, or the fork to the right? One path, you can put the pass behind you. The other, will only bring you pain and bondage, holding you back.

Do you know which path is which? When life here on earth ends, your journey will open to two doors. Will it be peace, or sadness? Will it be light, or darkness? What will it reflect, love or emptiness? If you have hatred, it's not for your neighbor. If you look closer, it's yourself.

Did you also waste your time, because there are no rewards for going left? Did you know you have choices, for how your story is told? Everyone has a destiny in Christ's eyes. Are you worthy, strong, wise with the strength and courage? Firstly, you are Christ's child, or if you choose left, your destiny will stand forever with scars, weariness, and forever untrustworthy.

Tell me, when you leave this earth, who will knock on your door? Who will guide you home? You have to know these scars are what we make them. Life on earth teaches lessons every day. For me personally, I received lots of lessons. You choose to learn, or not to learn. All chains have keys to their locks, and the only lock Smith, to call is Jesus. That's the only way to freedom!

When your story is told, and reading it out loud, will it tell a story of pride and honor? You know, Christ covers the pages. Is your story righteous, and printed with love? This happens, only if you choose to go right. God will create a song which will be played for you. God's children have their own song, and your past is put in the ocean.

Your past is put back from whence it came, and forgotten. Your history thus begins a new chapter. With Christ's blessing, love becomes a new home, covered with peace. We may leave, but Christ's love is always our protector. That gives us, always a safe home. History tells these stories offend. Remember, your thoughts matter, because your mind plays a big part in how you are presented to Christ. When you take a stand, what will be written? Will it be about the stand you took? Was it righteous, with an open heart, and a flag of peace, facing your enemy?

With Christ's love you will never be that lonely sailor, looking for a home. When sailing blindly, you have to know this: When you stare evil in the eye, remember he will be staring right back at you. Will you chose Christ or darkness? Will evil ever hear the voice of glory, with trumpets sounding in the back ground, or will he hear the song of death? Our history never sleeps, it's always on record. It is waiting for a story to be told.

Later, history records our battles, and how they were fought. That includes the battle at the mountain, and fire at your back. History shows you fought and won against the giant.

Along the way, emptiness tries to overtake you, but failed because you refuse to turn back.

This is what history will tell, if you are righteous. I hope, when your story is told, you stood with courage of Christ, and the faith of the Holy Ghost. Yes, everything past and present, is part of God's plan. Believe me, your story will be told. Did you know it goes back from the time you were born? It's not only the beginning, but how you ended life.

You must ignore things that are not in God's commandments. These things are only important in man's world. Under Christ, what do you have to offer from your inner self? What songs will you sing for His Grace? I only hope songs from the heart, with no off-key notes.

When you give your all, never be afraid, because you come with the army of Christ. Your enemy hears the trumpets blaring behind you. We always look for the face of Christ in our eyes. History can tell great stories of a servant, so loyal to Christ. In this story, history recounts those who are strong, destroying evil. Did you know history will write, and tell of your stand, if you choose to go right? History also teaches us what is to the left. On the left, there is fear and darkness, with ugly scars filled with shame. Secondly, they never see the light, and never stand, but crawl in bondage, there is no room to stand. You have no courage or strength. As we began to map out our life, let's remember there can be no dreams or hopes without Jesus.

For those none believers, standing in nothingness, they may not move back, or forward. They're not really evil, but not good. These souls are lost, and don't know it. They also don't step aside for progress. They just exist, which is a lonely place. In your daily planner, does Jesus name come up, and why do you need a planner?

Jesus Christ should always be a part of your life, planner or no planner. If we, plan our lives, we really are lost. If we continue to stay in the middle or on the left side, remember, only the righteous will inherit the riches from heaven. Do you think, if you stay in the middle, you're safe? No! You're not! Why?

You have to sing your loyalty. Stand on the right, were the fruit of your labor counts. We have choices. Freedom is standing to the right. When the **"Author"** writes the story of your life, will it be one of sorrow, or joy? We are taught what the right path is to reach Jesus.

You have to know this, no man can change the path God has set, only Christ determines your destiny. What you can control is your story. That's easy, righteous or evil. When you fail to believe in God, don't think shades on the windows, or close doors, will block the view. Remember, God takes care of the man that's homeless and hungry. He is also with the hungry, abused child, besides, women mistreated by a love one, or stranger.

Again, history records all, the good, the bad, and the ugly. What's important, is the words spoken, and actions taken. What lessons have we learned? Beware of the tongue, it is part of living and dying. Truth always wins, because when you lie, it's not just once.

Lies multiply to protect the first one, and so on. When your story is told, will someone open the windows of truth, or the door of your lies? Life is not guaranteed, unless we work for it. I want a history full of hopes, and dreams to inspire someone, and to continue to be blessed. I wish to inspire courage for all, as they reach for heaven.

Get to know Jesus. My history is not perfect, but my ending will be with Christ. I'm encouraged with that. My life is a working progress, no job goes unrewarded. However, there are times life can be brutal. With wisdom, and the cloth of Christ, it does not break me.

We relinquish things that are of the worlds possessions. This helps relieve the burdens on our shoulders. Positive things are still part of my history. We also need to pass to our young, setting their path to the journey to Jesus. In constant prayer, their history will be of the righteous. I'm not sure why, but history teaches us all darkness is not always evil.

In so doing, we learn to appreciate the light of Christ more every day. Day by day, as we go forward creating history, we find life takes and takes. When God gives you wisdom, you than know how it works. Our lives are sometimes filled with scars.

What can make the differences? Is it how you react to it? If there are scars, it only affects the unbelievers. When you're under God's wing, there are no scars. Did you know, sometimes history takes a pauses? It's only a few seconds, but it's exactly what you need, if you repent. You can write what's needed to record in history. The joy and love under your name is yet to be known.

When this pause happens, it's only for a second or two. Champion your heart, and reach for God. Do you understand history? Despite the pauses, it still offers everlasting life though God. **Repent!** Why not make God the center of your being?

Reading history, God took His time with man. This as well, as making the earth, with the flowers, animals, blue sky and oceans. He added one more cup of love. Loyalty is as important as the cup of wisdom, and two cups of blessings. Later, He added a special ingredient, making the world complete. What was it? **<u>Man and Woman!</u>**

We are different sizes and colors, and a sprinkle of joy for laughter. This definitely completes the world, so man can walk and breathe in Christ. Believe me, there are no artificial ingredients. If you are an unbeliever, you have no color or shine. Those ingredients are artificial, and a twist of lemon, when standing to the left.

God made you, and all man, by hand. His tool was love. He gives wisdom to all, under one roof. I know we say "neighbor"' but if you look closer. **"We Are Family."** With love, we should all move in one direction. Unbelievers need to catch up.

When I began researching history, I found I have been going place to place, searching for the beginning which had been lost in history. I look forward to the ending.

God knows I have sin. I have also brought scars to my love ones and neighbors. I'm here today to ask forgiveness and guidance. I'm hoping Christ finds me worthy. I once knew, that the path I was on, was not the one God set for me. I caused distractions with lies and deceit. I realized I was only fooling myself. God knows all, down to the last detail.

When I spoke with lies, it was only to myself. What I did was not honorable, under God. I found, what I was doing was only shorting my life. I only felt emptiness and sorrow, beyond measure. My goal in life is peace and joy, with a strong mind. I also need to have the strength of courage, and a loving heart. This comes from being well nourish from the soul, and wisdom to the spirit. All of this was needed for my goals in life.

I hope history records all of this. More important, this is the story I want told! When history reveals my story, I hope the light is shining, to inspire someone. This is how you are judged.

Stop! Step to the right, and have a new beginning with Christ.

God Bless!